YOUR BREAKTHROUGH IS UP TO YOU

YOUR BREAKTHROUGH
IS UP TO YOU

W. Nikki Pearson

Quoted scriptures are taken from various versions of the Holy Bible.

ISBN: 0692920609
ISBN-13: 9780692920602
Library of Congress Control Number: 2017911610
Nikki Pearson Publishing, Upper Marlboro, MD

Contents

Acknowledgments vii

Foreword ix

The Story xi

Introduction xiii

1 We've All Got a Story 1

2 If It Ain't One Thing, It's Another 22

3 When Hope and Faith Collide 38

4 You're on the Right Road Now 54

   The Last Mile of the Way 73

5 The Last Mile of the Way 75

Breakthrough 91

Author Biography 93

Acknowledgments

I would like to express my gratitude to my family and all those who've spent endless hours with me on this journey while writing *Breakthrough*. Doug, Sherreill, Michele, Gail, Veronica, Alberta, JoJo, and Chaplain Carr, thank you for reading, proofreading, and listening to me talk about *Breakthrough* endlessly.

Thanks Pastor John K. Jenkins, Sr., First Lady Trina Jenkins, the Women's Ministry team, and the First Baptist Church of Glenarden family, for your love, encouragement, and support. You are the wind beneath my wings.

Dr. Willie and Dee Jolley, thank you for believing in my dream for Breakthrough from the very beginning. Thank you for not giving up on me. You wouldn't let me give up.

Special thanks to Pastors Anthony E. Moore and Billy T. Staton Jr. for dialoguing with me about the Word, encouraging me when I felt insecure, and holding me accountable to do what I said God called me to do. You are my beloved brothers-in-Christ.

Thanks to my Create Space team for making this a smooth process. Your editorial letters were the icing on the cake.

Most of all, I thank God, who is the orchestrator of it all. To Him, be all the glory, and honor, and praise.

Foreword

I've known Nikki Pearson for many years. She is an incredible singer, powerful speaker, and a very artistic entrepreneur, yet she comes from a challenging past. She struggled with issues that took her down paths of self-destruction and into deep valleys she barely escaped. But somewhere in the heat of battle, she heard the story of a woman who had suffered with an issue for twelve years. The woman's name is unknown, but millions know her story. She is spoken of in the Bible, as the woman with the issue of blood. That one issue caused problems in every area of her life. It was devastating. But one day she heard something that took her on a journey that led her right to her healing and breakthrough. Nikki studied this woman's story and discovered that she didn't have to stay in bondage to her issues either. Like that woman, Nikki took action! The result of these actions was a life changing breakthrough.

In this book Nikki shares their stories. I encourage you to read this book, and then reread it. You will laugh; you will cry, but most of all, you will be inspired. Make no mistake, this is an in-your-face book. At times, you will feel like Nikki is writing about your personal issues. But if you get a grip on the principles and the words she shares with you, I am certain that like the woman in the Bible, and like Nikki, you too will get to the place of great expectation and celebration. They got their breakthrough, and you can get yours too. Your breakthrough is up to you!

Dr. Willie Jolley

Best-selling author of *A Setback Is a Setup for a Comeback* and *Achieve Greatness…with an Attitude of Excellence!*

The Story

She is busy going about her day...nothing too unusual...well, maybe a little more bloating this time, and oh, the discomfort; her breasts feel like balloons ready to pop; her feet and hands are swollen, but she just puts it off to the summer humidity and pre-period stuff... but the cramps...she never had cramps pre-period.

Even though she pushes it off, somewhere in the deep recesses of her mind, she knows this time that this period will be different...it's been coming for months; the spotting, the breakthrough bleeding, the headaches, and the flow...when it does come, it is heavy...oh yeah, this is not going to be the norm...

Gosh, she hates this time of the month...unclean, they call it, call her and the countless other girls and women who have a period. It is the Levitical law; nothing can be done about it, no way to get around it.

Rushing...preparing her food and things to take with her, she knows this time is different; her isolation will be longer than her normal three to five days. Her kids and husband have her check herself as she moves about the house...such an inconvenience if the whole house has to be shut down...everyone would know.

A kiss and a hug for the kids and a kiss for the husband, but the hug for him...she tries lingering in his arms awhile longer, but he pulls away...assuring her as he always does that all is well. But she knows...she knows this time is different...she knows this time she will not return so quickly.

Suddenly she pulls away, and off she goes, tears sliding down her cheeks. "I love you," she whimpers.

They tease, "Oh Mom, you do this every month." But she knows, surely this time is different...she steps outside the house and closes the door behind her...

And a certain woman having an issue of blood for twelve years, when she heard about Jesus, said to herself, "If I may touch the hem of His garment, I know I will be made whole." *Mark 5:25–34*

Introduction

It is such a shame how one issue can negatively affect every area of a woman's life. I've seen it happen in the lives of women of various ages and social and economic status. Issues know no color, education, or religion. Simply put, issues don't discriminate, and they are not time sensitive. One issue can haunt, taunt, trip, and entrap you for years. Issues are constant, insistent, and have the propensity to invade every waking and sleeping moment of your life. They will cause you to go places you would normally never go and make you stay longer than you ever intended to stay. Issues will make you lose your sense of identity, your self-worth, and your sense of belonging, and if you're not careful, issues will make you lose your mind. Issues will make you settle, compromise, give in, and give up. Issues will push you to overeducate, medicate, and complicate the simplest thing. Issues will make you depressed and oppressed, and they will suppress all the good in you. Issues will have you feeling locked in, locked out, and locked up, mentally and physically. All this and so much more is just the nature of issues.

But I've come to tell you that you don't have to be enslaved to your issues. Don't run from them any longer. Don't keep trying to cover them up, and certainly, stop denying that you have issues.

This book describes the path the woman with the issue of blood took to get her breakthrough from an issue she had endured for twelve years. Within the pages of her story, I have weaved segments of my own story of over thirty years of bondage to an issue that began when I was a little girl, culminating on that fateful night when I got my breakthrough. I believe as you follow our journey, you too will not only find the way to get your breakthrough, but you will also discover that your breakthrough is up to you.

1

We've All Got a Story

The story of the woman with the issue of blood is amazing to me. I must admit that when I first read her story, I didn't quite get why it was such a big deal. We don't even know her name. The Bible describes her as "a certain woman" who had an "issue" of blood that lasted for twelve years. She spent all she had going from doctor to doctor hoping to be healed, but her condition grew worse. Ultimately, that one issue had a negative influence on every area of her life. But something happened: she heard something about Jesus, and whatever she heard encouraged her so much that she decided to do something she had never done before to get her healing. The Bible says that she decided to touch the hem of Jesus's garment, and her journey begins with her chanting over and over, "If I may but touch the hem of His garment, I know I'll be made whole." Her plan was risky. It could cost her her life, but if she didn't do anything, she would surely die. She sought Jesus, she touched His garment, and she was healed and made whole. She shared her story and went about her business. End of story. I know, you're probably thinking like I did when I read it: "Oh, OK, nice story. Good for her, but that happened over two thousand years ago. What has that got to do with me, with women today? What's to say women who read this book even believe in Jesus, and even if we do, Jesus ain't just walking around here on earth now." You're right, but upon further study, I found that her story goes beyond what we read in the pages of the Bible, and it is the unwritten story that intrigued me so much that I tell it every chance I get to anyone who will listen. I teach workshops about her story. And now I've written this book about it. Knowing her story has changed my life forever, and many times when I shared it with others, it changed their lives as well. I believe there is a life-changing message in it for anyone who has experienced the devastating effects that one issue can have over every area of your life.

The good thing about her story is that it is one of hope, although she is helpless. In it is a lesson of faith overriding fear and determination in the face of years of defeat. Ultimately, it is a message of triumph and transformation instead of tragedy, and it proves that you don't have to stay bound by the issue and the corresponding problems it has presented in your life, no matter how long you've had to endure it. Come with me as I journey through our stories. I believe you will discover, just as I did, that her story proves that if you want to be free of the issue and the problems it has caused, you can be. Your breakthrough is up to you.

WHERE IT ALL BEGAN

I've always had a passion for helping others. It still hurts me to the core when I ride down the street and see women who are obviously strung out on drugs and alcohol, homeless, selling their bodies to fill voids that will never be filled that way. How my heart breaks for those women and for the young girls who are sick in their bodies and sick in their minds, begging for money or food to eat and something to drink while neglecting to feed their broken spirits and lost souls that are riddled with the effects of issues that have overtaken their lives. I've literally seen women running when no one was chasing them, holding conversations with the voices that spoke in their heads. They had issues, evident and openly displayed for all to see.

Those scenes would haunt me day and night. Then one day, I read the story about the woman with the issue of blood. Although her situation was different, I realized through in-depth study of her story that my story and the stories of the many women I saw and met on the street, in clubs and in churches, slinging hamburgers, and running organizations meant that we were, in some regard, more alike than different. It opened my eyes to so much more than the natural eye could see. It would take me places I didn't want to visit, make me face people, places, things, situations, and myself in ways I cared not to. But in the end, there was healing, deliverance, and a profound breakthrough from years of pain, grief, regret, bitterness, jealousy, loneliness, low self-esteem, and so much more. The woman with the issue of blood got her breakthrough, I got mine, and I am writing this book for you so you can get yours too. Your breakthrough is up to you!

I don't know the exact day or time. I don't even remember the year, but after reading her story, each time I would see or encounter those women on the street, my desire to do something or say something to help them, to take the hurt away, only intensified. I have literally given them the clothes off my back, the shoes off my feet, my furniture, and my personal belongings. I've cooked food and fed them. I have even brought some into my home for shelter. I remember a time when some of my girlfriends and I tried to help a homeless mom and her teenage kids. We put them in a hotel and paid for them to stay there for a few months. We fed them, brought clothes for them, and provided for them, only to find they kept being lured back to living on the street. I came to realize that often issues associated with homelessness go far beyond not having a place to stay or to call your own. It is because of the underlying issues that homelessness can become a state of mind, an accepted lifestyle. Still, I believed that breakthrough was possible for them.

Other women I encountered had unresolved issues that had affected them physically, mentally, emotionally, economically, socially, and financially, often all at the same time. Like so many of the others I encountered, they had been physically and/or verbally and emotionally abused at the hands of someone they loved and trusted. In other words, their problems were the by-product of an unresolved issue. Many I spoke with wanted to be different, live different, and do better, but they didn't know how or where to begin. It took this woman's story to help me realize that most had hope that one day they could get a breakthrough, but they were stuck. I so desperately wanted them to know that in spite of how bad it looked or how bad they felt, they still had a choice. It was possible for a breakthrough.

I encountered women who'd been hurt by the church and were spiritually wounded and/or lost. I met women who believed their lives started and ended in the five to ten blocks of their neighborhoods. They settled in to it, living with the negative effects of their issues, problems, hurts, and disappointments as if it were the norm. Still others sought help and were connected to government social services agencies, church benevolence programs, and nonprofit organizations, but for some reason and no matter what they tried to do, things just seemed to only get worse. They all had a story. In despair, I would cry out, "God, I want to help them. How can I help them?"

I'd hear the voice of God speak to me so clearly, saying, "You can help them. Tell them the story." I didn't realize then that the story would be more than that of the woman with the issue of blood, but it would be my story too. Ultimately, helping them would mean helping myself as well. I spent so many years of my life bound by the issues that threatened to take my life—and almost did. I too needed a breakthrough. I started telling the story.

I developed a five-week focus study based on the story of the woman with the issue of blood. While serving as the chaplain at a Salvation Army Drug and Alcohol Rehabilitation Center for men, I began sharing it with the residents and staff. The overwhelming response to that workshop was like nothing I could have imagined. For weeks, many of the men came to my office to talk about their hidden issues. I listened, I felt their pain, I heard their fear, I cried with them, I prayed for them, and I embraced them with all the love and compassion in me. I watched them as their lives began to turn around. The workshop was so successful that I was asked to present it as the keynote speaker for a conference at a local women's correctional facility. When I walked away from that event, I knew God had given me something that would be life changing for the many men and women I would encounter along my life's journey. To this day, I still hear stories of healing and breakthrough from the men and women who attended those events.

As a frequent guest speaker at some of these faith-based programs, I would often see the same faces week after week. Some sang with the praise team, while others smiled and greeted people coming in the door. But their eyes showed a different picture: signs of pain, fear, rejection, and more. Some of them even shouted and danced in the services; clearly, I could see they felt better. But the problem was that they did not get better. They were stuck in the grip of their issues.

As I looked at their body language and into their faces, I could see an image of how I had been: lonely, hurting, confused, and knowing I needed to change, that my entire life needed a change, but I didn't think I deserved better, and when I tried to make my life better, it seemed that things only got worse. I saw those women doing what I too had done for a while; they were running back and forth to the church because they got all excited hearing about what God could do and what He had done for others. But then they would go back outside the doors of the church, looking in all the wrong places and faces for their breakthrough and never finding it. You see, like me, they wanted it so badly, but they just could not believe or even imagine that the great God of the universe cared about them. I cried out on many occasions, "God, help me to help them." I would hear that voice so clearly say to me, "Just tell them the story." That's exactly what I've been doing, and I've seen breakthroughs begin to happen for so many.

ISSUES DON'T DISCRIMINATE

That is not the only group of women I've experienced this with. I told you issues don't discriminate. Anyone can have issues. I have taught workshops at church retreats and conferences. I have heard several women's stories that made my issues and problems look like I had simply dropped my bubble gum. I'm talking about women who were overseeing churches; women on the "preaching circuit"; women who were married with children, who had degrees, and who were living in mansions. However, after the doors of the church closed, they were overcome by the harsh reality that they preached healing and breakthrough but were living in hell themselves. They were trapped, bound to hurts and failures of the past that had progressed into ulcers, high blood pressure, cancer, nervous breakdowns, diabetes, depression, obesity, perverted sexual intimacies, frigidness (yes, I said it), and more. Some were in marriages that were just in name only because they had issues of being alone and lonely, so they got married for all the wrong reasons, and they ended up being lonely anyway—with a husband, kids, a dog, a hamster, and a waiting congregation. I heard a woman cry as she spoke of having an affair with the bishop, but after a while, he asked her to do him a favor, and he shared her with his friend. She thought she was living high because they kept her in luxury cars, a well-furnished condominium, expensive vacations, and designer clothes and shoes. But her tears were from holidays spent alone and birthdays spent with the girls, while the "big boys" were with their wives or the women they were planning to marry. One even told her that she wasn't the kind of woman that Christian men marry, but she would always be a great mistress. She believed him.

These women were praising God on the outside, but beneath the degrees and career positions, behind the makeup and clothes, luxury vehicles and jewelry, and prescription pain pills, they were silently dying on the inside. Several openly admitted they had turned to alcohol for solace, but all they got was drunk and a hangover. They were victims of low self-esteem and false pride, and they spoke of being full of regret, resentment, and unforgiveness. One moment they would be so nice, and yet the smallest incident would cause a rage to rise up that was so deeply embedded in them that it left no one standing.

EXPOSED

Now, I know right here that I need to say something: I am by no means judging any of the women I speak of in this book, as so many of their struggles are a part of my personal story too. Please know this book is not about judgment. This book is about a journey—a journey to break through. I am simply pulling back the covers, pulling off the masks, and exposing how any woman can be a victim of an issue, no matter her age, color, race, creed, and status in the community, from the church house, to the crack house, to the White House. No woman is exempt. Issues don't discriminate. We all have a story.

What I want you to know is that while I was being exposed to all this, God was beginning to expose me. I was so intimidated by these women, as I was suffering with my own issues of rejection, abandonment, low self-esteem, and need to be chosen first. I have a story.

My issue began when I was just a little girl. By the time I was three, my mom and dad had divorced, and my mom was remarried and had another daughter. My dad remarried also, and he too had another daughter. He visited me every now and then, but after a few years, he just stopped coming. It was during that same period that things started to really go downhill for me at home. My mom knew how heartbroken I was, but what made it worse was her obvious disdain for my dad. Consequently, she was fine with my dad not coming around. My heart broke to see her loving interactions with my stepdad and sister. It was like fuel on a fire. My sister and I began to fight often, as I became needy and sought their love and attention. I was jealous of their relationship, which only complicated things. I was just a child; I didn't understand. Then the unspeakable happened: Mommy witnessed someone touch me inappropriately. I was an innocent little girl who had been violated by a drunken adult, but shortly thereafter, her choice was to send me away to live with my grandparents, which hurt and confused me. I wondered for a long time what I had done wrong to make these bad things happen to me. Nobody told me why my daddy never said good-bye or why he did not come back. Mommy saw things happen to me and rather than console me, she scolded me and sent me away. I was devastated. I felt abandoned by my daddy, and I felt rejected by my mommy. I began to think something was terribly wrong with me. As much as my grandparents tried to convince me that my parents did love me, I didn't believe it. After all, my sister was still with them, and my other sister and daddy and her mom were together. It wasn't until much later in my life that I found out that the things that happened to me were not my fault. But by then, my life had spiraled out of control. I was an innocent little girl who took the brunt of bitterness and unforgiveness from a host of adults who had issues. Unfortunately, that would hurt and haunt me for many years.

It would be quite a while before I'd see my sister, my mommy, and my stepdad again. But when I did get to visit them on the weekends, it was so painful. It was blatantly clear how tightly knit the three of them were. I really loved my sister so much, but my issues of abandonment, rejection, and low self-esteem, coupled with the fact that time and distance stole our sisterhood, made me compete with her for my mom's attention. I can admit now that I often acted out to get my mom's attention. I took the fussing and even the whippings from her and my stepdad, but it got her attention. I cry even now as I write this. It was a very painful time in my childhood. Again, that might not sound so harsh to you, but for me, it broke my little heart. The feelings of abandonment by my dad and rejection from my mom negatively affected me throughout my childhood and late into my adult life. For so long, my life's song was "seems like I gotta do wrong before they notice me" (The Whispers, 1987).

My solace was that I did indeed love living with my grandparents. I loved them sometimes more than life itself. They were humble, giving, and full of love and compassion for everyone. They raised me in a healthy household and practiced and taught me the principles of God's Word. I was disciplined, and I was rewarded. I was encouraged, nurtured, and showered with love. I had cousins who lived on the same property and the neighbor's kids next door to play with. I loved them so much and was happy on the surface, but often, I became envious because they all lived with their parents and siblings. I found myself creating situations with them to force them to choose me over one another. Still, living with my grandparents and being around my cousins was the best place for me. I know that now, but the circumstances and situations that led to me being with my grandparents were my downfall. (More of my story later.)

I was telling the story, but because of my own issues, I was so intimidated by those powerful women I encountered and ministered to. I was intimidated by their status, their relationships, their ministry gifts, and their material wealth and possessions. Somehow, in all those experiences and in those I will speak of later, God was preparing me for something I was not quite ready to handle at that time, but with each experience, my story and this book were unfolding.

How did I know that, you ask? Only because I would still hear that voice so distinctly saying to me, "You can help them too. Tell them the story."

Write this down: "It is often in our struggles where our purpose is revealed, defined, and refined, and we are prepared to live the life we were created to live, with the knowledge, wisdom, strength, and grace to do it. Without a test, there would be no testimony."

ISSUES ARE NOT TIME SENSITIVE

I've met with women whose issues, like mine, began long ago, while others experienced theirs more recently, but in talking with each of them, their situations seemed like a lifetime. Maybe you can relate.

Perhaps you remember the day vividly: you got the answer wrong, and the teacher told you in front of the class that you needed "special education." Everyone laughed and called you the "special bus girl." Because of that, even to this day, you are overly competitive and never satisfied. Everything with you is "may the best woman win," thus you compromise your morals and principles to be the winner. And you wonder why people, women in particular, do not want to be around you.

Perhaps you got pregnant as a teenager, and Big Mama told you no man will ever respect you or marry you. Now all your friends are married with children, and you're still single. There are no prospects in sight, and you've had several other babies since then. You still haven't accepted the fact that because he loves having sex with you and moved in with you doesn't mean he loves you or wants to marry you. He is verbally abusive to you and leaves the care of the kids up to you. Every now and then, he will even hit you. But you stay with him because you'd rather be with any man just to prove Big Mama was wrong. You know they know the truth, but you have lied to them and yourself for so long that you've come to believe your own lies.

You've accepted this as normal. Yet deep down inside, there is a longing for something more, something right, something real.

Perhaps you only had to hear it one time, and it felt like somebody was pulling your heart out of your chest. Surely a mother wouldn't speak to her little girl like that. Your mind played all kinds of tricks as you fought back the tears. You became withdrawn in school, set back, set up, and dropped out. Now you can't get a good job, all because of what she said. Why did your mama treat you so badly when you loved her so much? Now she's gone, and you can't get any answers, and it still hurts. You can't have a good relationship with other females because you just don't trust them. The worst part is that you have a daughter, and you treat her like your mama treated you. You've said "I'm sorry" so many times, but she doesn't believe you, just like you didn't believe your mom.

Perhaps he touched you. He was playful at first, but still, it made you uncomfortable. Then it was when people weren't looking. Everyone was asleep, and he was in your room and in your panties. You lay there with tears falling and your eyes wide open for fear of dying if you closed them. You'd see the shadow of your mama at your door and hope that this time she'd open it, call the police, and hurt him for hurting her little girl, but you'd just hear her sigh as her shadow disappeared and the lights in the hall went out again. Now you're in recovery again, a whore, a prostitute, homeless, begging for food and a place to stay, going from man to man and sometimes woman to woman. You were just a little girl. Why did he do it? Why did she let him?

Perhaps you sit behind a big beautiful desk in a corner office with a window; your name is etched on the brass plate on your door. You've got the long title and a position that brings with it a great salary. "I deserve it; I sacrificed a lot to get here" is what you constantly tell yourself. Yes, it's taken you years of *serving* him to get to this place. You were still there for him long after others had punched the clock. Now you see the pretty young thing sitting where you used to sit, his new receptionist. She's ambitious and hungry for success and status just like you were, and he preys on that vulnerability in a woman. You know the routine: now she will serve him coffee, and later she will just *serve* him. It's only a matter of time before he will move her into your office and move you out.

Perhaps they sent you away. They told everybody you were going to help take care of your auntie who was sick. A year later, you were back home, but your auntie, who wasn't really sick, is raising your baby as her own. Now with an abortion under your belt, you have finally met a man who loves you and wants to marry you and have children, but you're too scared and ashamed to tell him about your past. So you stay single and childless when all you ever really wanted is to be loved and married with children.

The stories I could tell you are endless, but I think you get the point. Any woman, young or old, can have an issue, and issues can start at any time, multiply, and go on for years.

Finally, after several years of preaching, teaching, and telling the story, I felt compelled to write this book. But writing this book has been one of the hardest things I have had to do thus far in my life. I learned that I could not lead people to a place if I was not willing to go there myself, and that my personal story is the foundation of the years of preparation to write this book. Writing this book forced me to confront my own personal issues and all the problems associated with them. I learned firsthand that you will never get a breakthrough if you deny you have an issue. You've got to deal with it. I heard someone else say it like this: "You cannot conquer what you are not willing to confront, and you can't fight it if you don't face it." The woman with the issue of blood did not deny that she had an issue, and as we will see later, for twelve years, that one issue affected every area of her life. It made her an outcast from her family, friends, church, and mainstream society. How do we know she didn't deny it? In Mark 5:26, we read that for twelve years she went from doctor to doctor trying to get healed, trying to get her breakthrough.

If you are serious about getting a breakthrough from the problems those issues have caused in your life, then you absolutely cannot act like they do not exist. For the most part, that means addressing the source of the issue in the first place. Let me explain it this way, with a true story.

Not long ago, I began to have some discomfort in my right side. At first, I just shoved it off as the result of too much ice cream or some fibrous concoction that had given me gas. Then after a couple of weeks, bowed over in pain, I went to the emergency room. I was in so much pain that before the actual diagnosis, the ER physician immediately wanted to give me pain and gas medication, but I refused. In all that pain, I said no meds, at least not yet. I know you people with low pain tolerance are gritting your teeth, but my thing is to get to the source of the pain before we kill the pain. Good thing I said no. I learned from the doctor that night that we may have pain and complications in one area, but the source of the pain may come from another area. I was hurting up under my rib cage, but the final diagnosis was a bladder infection.

And that's the way it is with issues and problems. They all have a root, a starting point, but if we focus only on the pain they cause, we'll just keep getting the pain prescription refilled but never heal or get rid of the cause of the pain. That's what needs to be dealt with so that you can get healed and never feel that pain again.

For those of you who have been bamboozled into thinking that if you don't admit having an issue that you actually have then somehow the issue will just disappear, I'm telling you that is ludicrous. Deal with your issue. Don't deny it.

I understand that your issue may not be like the woman in the Bible or issues like mine. Your issue may be fear, shame, regret; it may be feelings of being unworthy, of being unloved, of not fitting in, or of being too thin or too fat, too short or too tall, or any number or combination of things. Your issue may be the result of something someone said to you, and you still hear it resonating in your ears every day and night. Perhaps your issue is the result of something someone did to you that left invisible scars, but you still feel the piercing pain as if it just happened yesterday. Or maybe your issue is self-inflicted, or maybe it is none of these. But whatever it is, if you have read this far, then I believe it's your time and your turn for a breakthrough. I cannot tell you that it's going to be easy or quick, but I can assure you that the pain to change will not be greater than the pain you will experience if you choose to remain the same.

AND WHEN YOU PRAY...

A few of the women I have spoken to said they started out praying, but when they didn't get what they prayed for by a certain time, they got discouraged. Many said they just weren't sure if prayer really works. Truth be told, from time to time, I have felt that way too. But what kept me praying, at least every now and then, was the image of my granddaddy getting on his knees every night and praying. Granddaddy would say, "Nikki, God will do His part. You do yours." So yes, by all means pray. I suggest reading the Gospel of Matthew 6:5–13 to learn the pattern of prayer. And although it is true that God may not come when you want Him, I can tell you with all certainty that He will show up in His time. Pray the scriptures and believe what you pray for. Pray!

DO SOMETHING OUT OF THE ORDINARY

The woman with the issue of blood was determined and would not be held up by tradition, pride, or the social and legalistic norms of the day. She didn't have a normal issue, so she needed an abnormal plan. Getting your breakthrough may mean doing something out of the ordinary, taking risks. What works for everybody else may not work for you. You cannot continue doing the same thing over and over again and expect different results. That is insanity. Don't be afraid to take healthy risks. If you want something different, then you must take the risk and do something different to get your breakthrough.

YOU MUST BE DETERMINED

You must be determined. I got tired of trying, I got tired of praying, and a few times, I just outright fell. But I did not stay down, and I did not give up. At times, I couldn't even see my way. Sometimes it looked like things were getting worse instead of better, but every time I read and heard this woman's story, it gave me hope—it stirred up and increased my determination. Don't give up. Your breakthrough is up to you!

ARE YOU SICK AND TIRED YET?

Before you go any further, I must ask you, are you tired of being stuck? Are you tired of covering up your issues and problems, denying that they even exist? Are you tired of spending all your money on clothes, weaves, makeup, and "stuff" just to end up looking great on the outside while feeling ugly and broken on the inside? Are you tired of the yo-yo spin of feeling good one day and then like you want to die the next, all the while smiling and laughing on the outside, but on the inside, there is a war going on? Let's face it: once you wash the makeup off and get undressed, your issue is still there. It doesn't have to stay like that.

Are you losing sleep because you're staying up all hours of the night studying for another degree? You can solve scientific equations and run a nonprofit like a Fortune 500 business, but you're stuck when it comes to solving your own personal issues and problems.

Are you done with sticking your key in the door of a beautiful mansion that has never been a home because it lacks genuine love, laughter, and peace? Don't get me wrong: there is nothing wrong with looking good and having nice things. And there is absolutely nothing wrong with getting higher education or owning a beautiful house. But there is something wrong when you're doing these things only to cover up and not deal with your issue and problems. How much education and how many designer clothes, purses, and pairs of shoes have made your issue go away? How does it feel living in that large house while you are haunted day in and day out by your issues?

And you, dear lady, have become a joke in your own home. Aren't you tired of your kids making light of your issues? On top of that, your husband seems to leave earlier and earlier, go out more and more, and stay away longer and longer. All night you continue to scream, but you do it in silence while tears flow like a rushing waterfall down your cheeks because in the real sense, although you are living on the inside, it really feels like you're on the outside looking in. I declare there is a breakthrough for you if you want it. I know personally that God can turn those tears of pain and sorrow to tears of joy. He can turn your mourning into dancing (Psalm 30:11).

And what about you, my sister? Are you sick and tired of being sick and tired, of living from pillar to post, from shelter to shelter? Are you tired of going from man to man, and more recently, from woman to woman, because you'd rather be with anybody than deal with your issue of neglect and the fear of being alone or lonely?

Get real here with me: Are you tired yet? Are you really ready to throw away the bottle and the drugs and to get free once and for all? It's your choice as well. I declare to you too that your breakthrough is up to you.

For fifteen years, I tried drinking, drugging, and sexing my issue away, but it was a false sense of healing and a terrible way of escape; all of it was just a temporary fix. I always ended up right back where I started. I moved from lover to lover, feeling in love but never really loving in a healthy way and never really being loved in a healthy way. (Let me remind you again that just because a man continues to have sex with you does not mean he loves you or even cares!) Since I'm telling all my business, the real deal is that I was unable to receive real love because I didn't even love myself. I bet someone reading this book can relate.

NOW IS THE ACCEPTABLE TIME

Whoever you are, wherever you are, I don't care what it looks like, I don't care what it feels like—this is not all there is for you. If you've read this far, I believe with all my heart and faith that within these pages lies the fuel to stir up your hope and ignite the fire of faith and determination that will lead you through to your breakthrough— that is, living a life free from the bondage of your past issues and the problems they've created, however long ago that was.

This is the time to call your issue out for what it is and acknowledge that it happened, that it hurt and perhaps still hurts, but that you are still alive, God has not let you die from it, and today He is giving you the opportunity to move toward your healing and total well-being. Yes, I do declare that your breakthrough is on the way. It's up to you.

If you are really ready for this, it begins right now. It will work if you work it! I feel your apprehension, maybe a little doubt, and that's OK. I understand. This is not about putting your trust in me. Yes, I have the experiences, and I certainly have the story and testimony, but I am just a witness. Put your trust in God. You can rely and depend on Him (1 Peter 5:7). Take a moment and read the following text out loud: "With people things are impossible, but with God all things are possible" (Matthew 19:26). There is absolutely nothing too hard for God (Jeremiah 32:17).

It's your choice. If you don't know, then let me be the one to tell you: you have the ability and the right to choose this day, this very moment, to either stay stuck or to move forward and to get your breakthrough. Get a different perspective on your situation. That's right, in spite of what it looks like, and how you feel, God created you on purpose and instilled in you a divine purpose, a destiny just waiting for you to walk in it. (Read Psalm 139:13, 16.) Please know that you are not alone. And let me say this: just because you don't know your purpose does not mean you don't have a purpose. Yes, you do! Are you with me? Are you ready for your breakthrough? I'm telling you, you got this. Your breakthrough is up to you!

JUST FOR YOU

To help guide you and strategically move you along, at the end of each chapter, you will find questions and/or exercises for you to respond to. Do not enter into this with any preconceived thoughts of what you should or should not say or do. Relax. There are no expectations other than you being honest with yourself. I suggest you read at a pace that is right for you. Notice I did not say a comfortable pace. Sometimes facing the truth, confronting your issues, and dealing with things that have been wrong for so long is uncomfortable. It may hurt, but the rewards of a breakthrough far outweigh the momentary pain of being honest. If you feel the need to, don't hesitate to ask someone whom you admire and trust to stand with you on this journey. This person could be a social worker or counselor, a sibling, a relative, a clergy member, a prayer partner, or someone who wants to see you succeed in life. I just ask that you be consistent. Don't hesitate to read a chapter over if you think you missed something. This is not a race to see how fast you can get to the end of the book or get your breakthrough. Besides, two factors are set. First, the book does have an ending, a happy ending, and second, whether it happens now or much later, your breakthrough is still up to you. I have also included encouragement quotes, basic life principles, and even scriptures along the way. Read them every chance you get, and speak them out loud to yourself until they drown out the negativity and noise in your head and heart. The Bible teaches us in Proverbs 18:21 that life and death are in the power of the tongue. If you want life, then speak life. If you want to be healed, then start speaking healing. If you want a breakthrough, then begin speaking breakthrough. Believe it; God's Word is truth, and when you begin to speak His Word, it starts to manifest (Isaiah 55:11). Don't hesitate to find out what the Word of God says about a particular thing, and speak it. Here in this book, I have paved the way, but you must take the steps. Your breakthrough is up to you.

May I pray for you? *God, You are the awesome and mighty God who created everything. You know each of us by name, and You are aware of all our situations, the good and the bad. You know our innermost secrets, and God, You know the consequences of the things said or done to us as well as the things we have said and done to ourselves and/or to others. Yet You have not let us die, and You have given us this chance to make a change in our lives. Thank You. I pray for Your strength and guidance for those reading this book. I ask that You remove all their fears and doubts, bitterness, anger, resentments, and unforgiveness. And God, fill them with Your love and Your power. Give them sound minds that are full of knowledge and wisdom. God, present the opportunities for them to hear Your Word that meets them right where they are, that will instill hope and faith in their hearts and give them a sense of Your peace and presence. I pray that You slay every attack and attempt of the devil whenever he tries to discourage and detain them and that You use it in them as fuel for their determination to get their breakthrough. Thank You that in spite of all the hurt and pain* *and confusion, nothing in our lives goes to waste; You use every trial and test, every fall and failure, so that You are glorified, and we are better and not bitter. You get all the glory and honor. In the name of your son, Jesus, I pray. Amen.*

REFLECTION: WE'VE ALL GOT A STORY

1. What's your story? What happened to you? What was said? What was done?

2. What is your issue or issues?

3. The following scriptures are to encourage you as you confront your issue. Read them out loud; make it personal. What does the Bible tell us about trials (trouble)?
   - James 1:2-3: "Consider it pure joy, my brothers, *whenever you face trials* of many kinds, because you know that the testing of your faith develops perseverance."
   - Isaiah 54:17: "No weapon that is formed against you will prosper."

Journal. Now that you know there is purpose in our trials and pain and that you will triumph over them, use this time to write your thoughts.

Nothing in your life goes to waste. God uses it all to make you better.

2

If It Ain't One Thing, It's Another

One issue caused so many problems for this woman that it affected every area of her life. We know from the story that she spent all she had running from doctor to doctor seeking a cure while her condition just grew worse. Her body was breaking down, and she was also financially broke. What started out as physical also became financial.

Her issue affected her in the areas of intimate and social relationships, because in her day, having an issue meant you were classified and treated as unclean. She was ostracized from the general population, and yes, even from her family. If she was married, she could not have any physical contact with her husband. As a matter of fact, she could not hug or touch anyone, and that included her children, if she had any. It's possible that she would have had to leave her husband, her children, and her home. Her husband could divorce her if he chose to. Her issue made her untouchable.

Having the issue that long probably affected her mentally and emotionally; she lost her identity, as people no longer addressed her by her name. That was bad, because names meant something in those days. It was a foretelling of your occupation, your destiny, your inheritance, and your status in society. Instead, she was identified by her issue—*unclean*, they would call her. She would also have to announce herself as she entered mainstream society by crying out "unclean." It was in some ways like saying, "Here comes the misfit, unfit, sick, diseased, untouchable, unwelcome, and uninvited." She was ostracized, cast out of her home, and pushed away from the general public, with no comforting arms or words.

Her issue affected her spiritually. Being unclean meant she was looked upon as defiled and as unfit to participate in any ceremonial events. Besides the fact that she wasn't allowed in the general public areas, she wasn't even allowed to enter the temple to worship. Even the church folk turned their backs on her. I told you there was more to her story than meets the eye.

LET'S ASSESS THE DAMAGE

It blows my mind every time I think about how just one issue can cause multiple problems. Several dictionaries define the word *issue* as a constant flowing. In other words, it's there all the time. When you wake up in the morning, it's there. As you go about your day, it's there. And it is still there when you go to bed at night. It literally becomes one thing on top of another. It affects you physically, emotionally, financially, and spiritually. I know this from personal experience. It affected me in every area of my life.

My issues of rejection and abandonment flowed over into my relationships with everybody. I became insecure and clingy and always feared that people either did not love me or would stop loving me and send me away or leave me. As a child, I was never far from my grandmother's side, and I didn't want her out of my sight for long. And my granddaddy really caught hell with me. (I can say this now with a tear and a smile.) He used to say I followed him foot to foot. Well into my preteen years, when Granddaddy got up at the crack of dawn to go get the chicken eggs, I was with him. When he took out the cows, fed the hogs, and plowed the land, I was out there with him. When he got in his truck to drive the thirty-five miles into the city for choir rehearsal, I was sitting in that raggedy old truck right beside him. He'd teach me the words and harmony parts of the songs, and we'd sing going to and coming from rehearsal. (He was planting seeds, and we didn't even know it.) When I couldn't go with him, I felt rejected and abandoned all over again. But it got worse as my relationship insecurities rolled over into my childhood friendships and beyond. I needed to know that someone cared enough about me so that if given a chance to choose between me and another person, they would choose me first. It did not help that for some reason my mom had adopted the thought that nobody really liked me, and from elementary school to well past adulthood, she frequently told me that. When I was little, she said people only wanted what I had: long black hair and nice clothes. As a teen, she said the same thing, and even as a young woman, she tried to convince me that none of my female or male friends meant me any good. This just compounded my issues of abandonment and rejection. Any self-esteem I had was at the bottom of the barrel. My insecurities fueled my quest to prove her wrong. Consequently, I would come between various best friends and boyfriend-girlfriend relationships among people I knew. It was never that I wanted to hurt anybody. It did indeed hurt me to know others were hurt, but still, I relished that false sense of importance when I was chosen first over another. I just wanted to know what it was like to be chosen first. (God would deal with me about that.)

At nineteen years old, I met the man who would become the father of my only child. Right away he made me feel like I was the most special person, the only woman in the world for him. He was in the army, and when he came home on the weekends, we were inseparable. His family was large and exemplified in my mind what a family should be. They were always visiting one another or doing things together; the cousins were more like brothers and sisters to one another. Sure, they had their ups and downs and family fights just like any other family, but they always seemed to work things out. I was drawn to that as they so easily embraced me and treated me like one of their own. I started to feel and believe that others did genuinely like me and love me. His mom nurtured me and helped me see myself in a better way. She never failed to tell me that my parents loved me and that adults sometimes make decisions that are the best at the time but that children may never understand. She always encouraged me to love them.

My son's dad was stationed miles away. When he would have to return to the base or leave the country, he would write me long love letters. Can I tell you that my self-esteem rose to the top, as I often received more than two letters a week from him confessing his eternal love for me? I was happier than I ever imagined. I remember being at a wedding for one of his relatives, and as the bride and groom said their vows, we said them too. I disregarded my grandparents telling me not to move in with him without getting legally married first. I really loved him, and I was so naive and desperate for the kind of attention he showed me that I didn't listen to them. Unfortunately for me, that fairy-tale arrangement would not last long. Things changed between us when he got out of the service. By the time I realized I was pregnant, he was already intimately involved with someone else, and he moved out. The little self-esteem I had died, and I thought I was going to die. I wanted to die. My mom and grandparents were so disappointed and angry with me for being pregnant, unmarried, and abandoned. My mom was so angry and reminded me repeatedly that she told me he didn't care about me. That hurt me to the bone. My grandparents were so ashamed. I can't describe to you how I felt for disappointing them. The pain was beyond what I ever imagined having to endure. The eight-year-old little girl in me was rebirthed, and she stayed around a long time.

I was determined that after my son was born that his dad would come back to me and love us. I would show them all. He was living with that other woman, yet I still turned all my attention to trying to get him back. I learned years later how foolish I was and that I was living a fairy tale by thinking that because we had a son, it was the perfect reason for us to be together. Pursuing that relationship would become a mistake that could have cost us our lives. And it almost did.

Can you see how my issues moved beyond relational and became emotional and mental? But it didn't stop there.

We did start seeing each other again, but by then, he had his own place, and we were both dating other people. I still loved him and was obsessed with having him choose me first over the other women. It was so bad that I accepted in some regard all the other women, but I just wanted to be number one. I really believed that being the mother of his son meant we were supposed to be together as a family.

After a while, my issues affected me physically. I don't remember the first time he hit me, but the beatings became frequent. He would hit me and then promise never to do it again, but he lied, and it only got worse. Still, I kept going back, each time thinking it would be different. I feared being with him, yet I was scared of not having him in my life. I rationalized it all by thinking that at least I had somebody sometimes, and when it was good between us, it was really good. And I am not just talking about sex. So I stayed, all the time hoping that I would do or say something to make him love me like his letters said, to make him choose me over the other women. He stayed, and he left. He kept telling me he loved me and wouldn't do it again. It had been far too long by the time I woke up from that violent and dysfunctional fantasy merry-go-round. I should have left him the first time he hit me. Calling the police, having him locked up, and then going back to him only made the abuse worse. It became a seesaw for years. Finally, after broken bones, black eyes, a concussion, and my failed attempt to cause him serious bodily harm, we both knew it was time to walk away. By the time I stopped seeing him, my life had really spiraled out of control. My issues of abandonment, rejection, and wanting to be chosen first birthed emotional, mental, and physical problems that flowed in every area of my life, both day and night.

Please note that what he did was wrong. *No man should ever hit a woman.* If you are a victim of domestic violence in any capacity, get away, find safe shelter and counseling, and get help.

Although I was the victim of domestic abuse, as are some of you, please note that this is not why I shared that period of my life. I shared that with you to further show you how dealing inappropriately with the issues and problems in our lives can roll over into other areas. Look at what happened in my life.

Eventually all this led me to a life of heavy drinking and drug use and many unhealthy relationships and associations as I sought to medicate my deepest pain and turmoil. I took love or some semblance of it when and where I could get it. I didn't feel worthy of having such a beautiful baby boy, so I ended up sharing the raising of my son with my mom and stepdad while I chose to live my life still searching for significance and self-worth. I kept telling myself that once I was a famous singer, once I got that good-paying job, once I got my own car, and more nonsense, then somebody would choose me first, and then I could get my son, and we could be a family.

I'm telling you, issues will affect your mind and heart, and every part of your life can be challenged, changed, and negatively influenced by one unresolved issue.

IT GETS WORSE BEFORE IT GETS BETTER

All those things sent me down a long path and years of self-destruction.

For almost fifteen years, my life was consumed with singing or hanging in clubs, bars, parties, and cabarets. I was keeping busy singing with a few well-known local jazz bands and even formed a few bands myself with some of the finest musicians in the District of Columbia, Maryland, and Virginia. I was popular and had a few sugar daddies who kept me dressed in designer suits and shoes and driving nice cars. I thought I was living the life. But all of it was a false sense of positive change. Along with losing my self-esteem, I lost my self-respect and my identity. I was still trying to be the number-one choice in someone's life. I became who and what others called me and said about me or who I thought they wanted and needed me to be. I didn't know who I was anymore, and I found myself simply trying to fit in.

I was singing the blues, and still living the blues, while the daily and nightly supply of free cocaine, alcohol, and sex anesthetized my pain. By then, like Marvin Gaye sang, "I was flying high in the friendly sky." I kept going back to the place where the good feeling awaited me. Self-destruction was in my hands. I was so stupid minded.

It was during this crazy period of my life when my granddaddy died, and I was totally devastated. The only man who I knew really loved me was gone. My way of dealing with his death was burying myself deeper in short-lived relationships with men who I knew from the start would only be in my life temporarily. So after just a few weeks or months, I would end the relationship—after all, I was convinced they would eventually leave me anyway. My dad left me, my son's dad left me, and then my granddaddy died. I would continue that cycle of "love them and leave them" until I was well into my late thirties. Can you see how my issues became mental?

Eventually I went running back to the church. I started attending church regularly and singing with a choir as well as singing solo for church special events. The problem with that was I often saw men who were leaders in the church I attended at some of the clubs and bars where I was singing and partying. Several partied and danced with me on Friday and Saturday nights but then acted as if they didn't know me in church on Sunday. In church, many treated me as if I was the woman with the issue of blood, as if I was unclean. Other people in the church knew I had a baby out of wedlock and was singing in clubs, and I'd hear the comments they made about me when I was chosen to sing a solo or special selection. I smiled and was friendly toward them, but their words and attitudes toward me hurt, and slowly, I drifted away from the church again. I thought their behavior toward me meant I wasn't good enough. I was convinced that God didn't love me either. Cocaine, alcohol, fornication, adultery, and singing in clubs became my lovers, religion, and gods. But they were only temporary and ineffective fixes. So now on top of everything else, my issue affected me spiritually. The strange thing is that I believed in God. I believed in Jesus.

I started believing in God and Jesus when I was just a little girl. But like I said earlier, the problem was I could believe in God's love, blessings, and healing for everybody else, but I just couldn't believe in God for myself. I bet I got some witnesses on that.

When I think of it now, an issue is like a single snowflake that hits the snow-covered ground and begins rolling, gathering more snow, and leaving a path of problems and destruction as it descends. By the time it hits bottom, it has become a huge boulder. It seems like it will never melt. It happened with the woman with the issue of blood, and it happened for me. And it's happening for so many others, maybe even you. But I declare to you this moment that it doesn't have to end there; eventually, the sun will shine again, and that snowball will melt. The Bible says it like this in Psalm 30:5: "Weeping may endure for a night, but joy comes in the morning." OK, let me say it another way: trouble don't last always.

DIFFERENT STROKES FOR DIFFERENT FOLKS

Issues and the problems they create affect everyone differently as they take up our time, energy, emotions, and often, our resources. Many women are filled with shame and withdraw from family, friends, and associates. They stop hanging out, get depressed, isolate themselves, and more. Some simply fret and sweat, fuss and worry, but never attempt to seek and/or try to find a solution. Still others live in denial that the issue and problems even exist. But I learned the hard way that it is not healthy to simply ignore issues and problems because, for the most part, they will not just go away. Don't you see it now how issues and problems can be very damaging to every area of your life? That in turn rolls over into the lives of others in your circle or that you encounter. It is also not good to spend too much time focusing on issues without searching for the source and then the solution.

WE ARE STILL HERE!

Like I did, some will seek refuge in drugs and alcohol, promiscuity, and perverted sex. Some may even attempt to take their own lives. I too made that attempt several times, but I can tell you right here that God had another plan. How do I know that, you ask? Well, I am still here. Yes, I thank God. I know now that my issues and problems were not unto death, and I declare to you today that neither are yours. How can I say that? I knew you'd ask that question. The answer is the same: because you are still here.

ISSUES AND PEOPLE, OH MY

Some of us talk about our issues and problems to anybody who will listen. But for the most part, people get tired of hearing it. It hurts us when they say things like "Oh no, not again," and "Why does this keep happening to you?" and "You must be doing something wrong." Can we be honest right here? You start to believe that maybe you have been cursed.

Those of you who are Christians (Romans 10:9–10) have even asked the question, "God, am I really your child?" As if being a Christian makes you exempt from trouble. The Bible clearly lets us know that we are going to have trouble. I suggest you read what John 16:33 says. From the beginning of time, people had trouble. Adam and Eve had trouble. So don't think it's strange. Even so, friends and acquaintances have the nerve to look down on you and to tell you things like "Get yourself together; it ain't all that." And what's even more painful is when you know people see you coming, and they look the other way or say a quick hello and then dash for the nearest exit as if you are contagious. The thing is, in your heart, you know it's not that they don't care about you. I imagine for the most part at least some of them do. But it's your issue and all those problems—that's why they avoid you. Most are clueless as to why this is happening to you. Many have done all they are capable of and know to do to help you. Therefore, being around you makes them feel useless and helpless, and they walk away. Honestly, you know there is nothing they can do. Then again, your being around them makes you feel unwanted, and so you just stay stuck; you think you'll never measure up to anybody's standards. It seems like you'll never fit in. Even your well-intentioned best friends conclude that you must be committing some kind of unforgivable sin because nothing seems to be working in your favor. But please don't let people box you in or tie you down with their unfounded thoughts and opinions. I believe sometimes we just have to get delivered from people and their opinions.

For so long, I began to see myself the way I thought others saw me. Consequently, I treated myself badly because others did. As I got older, others treated me badly because I either allowed it or often invited it. Did I just say that? In this regard, I had to make another decision. I could either continue abusing myself and/or allow others to abuse me, or I could say enough is enough. The fact is that was hard for me to do. Bad habits are hard to break, especially when fueled by fear. You see, I was more afraid of being alone than I was of being physically, emotionally, and even verbally abused. Yet the crazy part is, somewhere deep inside of me, I knew the bad things people said about me were not true. I mean, I knew I was doing wrong, and wrong certainly had been done to me, but I was still a good person deep down inside. I was a giver. I was always looking out for someone else, encouraging someone else to think better, do better, live better. Young girls in the neighborhoods where I lived and even on my jobs liked hanging out with me, but I always, always told them to live better than I did. I was open and honest with them about my issues, and some tried to help me and to be there for me, but as many of you know, nobody can do for you what you are not willing do for yourself. Is it clear that it was never my intent to hurt anybody? I just had this issue where I needed to be the one chosen first, the one loved the most. Do you see the snowball effect happening?

Issues will take you places you never intended to go, make you be with people you never, ever planned to be with, and make you stay longer than you intended to stay. Did I say that before? It bears repeating. Not dealing with issues appropriately can make you blind to the truth. Are you willing to admit that today? You know the truth, you know what is right and what is wrong, but you still do it your way because you have convinced yourself that you are in control, and it is your way or the highway. But nothing is changing. Not you or your situation. The Bible is so right when it reminds us that there is a way that seems right to a person, but it is the pathway to destruction and death (Proverbs 14:12).

START SEEING THINGS DIFFERENTLY

At some point, we all must start a self-reflection. I imagine most of you already know that it generally does not feel good when we do a self-exam because it may mean seeing some things about our character and life that are ugly and painful. And we have to face it and accept the truth of what we see. It does not matter if the issue is self-inflicted or the result of something someone else did to us or said to us and/or about us—issues and the problems they create are hard to face. Yet if you're really honest with yourself right here, you should admit that it is getting harder and harder to ignore and cover it up. I know you're hurting and confused, and you're tired of things seemingly getting better only to find that they've actually gotten worse. You're desperate; you just need a breakthrough. I hear you cry, "When is it my turn? When will this be over? Will I ever get through this? Somebody, please help me!" Well, that's OK. Pull out the tissues. As you can see, I've had to do my share of crying and weeping, especially while writing this book. But now you know I could not tell the story if I had not lived much of it myself. I can write this book because like the woman with the issue of blood, I made it through. I got my breakthrough, and the good thing is, so will you. Your breakthrough is up to you.

DON'T GIVE UP

At times I thought I was losing my mind. Sometimes I thought I was going to die, and quite honestly, I wanted to die because there were moments when the pain, shame, guilt, confusion, and feelings of rejection, abandonment, and loneliness were much more than I thought I could bear. I went to doctors and psychiatrists who said I was depressed. They said it wasn't clinical but situational. Well, duh, I knew that, but it didn't help matters. Still, at one point, I was put on medication. In some regards, pills took away the feeling of depression, but they didn't take away the reality that my life was out of sync. There was no balance, and often, I didn't know what was fake or real. I felt awful with pills, and I felt awful without pills. I was a walking time bomb, and I should have died. Yet deep down inside of me, the soul of my being would not let me give up. And that made me at least wake up every day, even if I did not get up every day. I bet you know what that feels like, don't you? Yet in all that and in what I was going through, all the times I was in the wrong place, with the wrong person or people, doing the wrong things, God still let me live. At some point, that produced just enough hope in me to believe that just maybe, one day, I could get my breakthrough. Maybe one day someone would love and care for me enough to choose me first. I began to think that God must have something better for me. And you know what? God did, and He still does. And that same thing holds true for you. I say with much compassion and conviction that your issues are not there to take your life. Your issues are there to prepare you for a better life, to take you higher, and to make you wiser and stronger. So hold on, and hang in there. Keep reading, and you'll see.

HOW DO YOU SEE IT?

Something to keep in mind is that a lot of what we experience and how we respond to it is based on our personal perspective—that is, how we see a thing. Let me encourage you right here to try to look at things differently. We can start by knowing and applying this right here: the Bible says that God made us specifically unique, on purpose and with a purpose, and that none of us is an afterthought (Jeremiah 1:5, 29:11). As I began to believe that, my perspective started to change, and I began to look differently at my situations, myself, and life in general. I did not—could not—deny what had happened and was happening, but what I realized was when I started to look at it from a different perspective, it also changed how I responded to it. When I did that, I found strength I didn't know I had, the energy to keep trying, and the determination to keep pursuing my breakthrough, even if I made mistakes along the way. This right here bears repeating over and over again. I came to understand that all we go through, whether self-inflicted or brought about by others, is allowed in the process of time and is working together for the purpose for which we were created. Yes, there is pain in the process, but I could not sing or teach or preach or write this book so transparently with the conviction that I do if I had not experienced all that I have. You've got to change the way you see yourself, your situation, and life in general. I know what I am about to write is not proper English, but it is the truth: this here, what is happening in your life right now, it ain't all there is. This is not the end! I declare to you that there is a breakthrough with your name on it. Now is the time to change your perspective. Stand on your hope and God-given strength and determination, and don't you ever give up! Your breakthrough is on the way, and it is up to you.

IT'S NEVER TOO LATE: KEEP HOPE ALIVE
The woman with the issue of blood held on for twelve years. She had hope. She wanted and expected something to happen, which is why she kept going to physicians and spending all her money. Even when her money ran out, she held on. She still believed she could be healed. She would not settle for that situation, and she was

determined not to die in that situation with that issue and all the problems it caused her.

I struggled for over twenty-seven years. I was thirty-five years old when my life began to turn around. Make a note right here: it's never too late. I had hope. This woman had hope. She believed she could be healed, and that's why she spent all she had. I too believed that one day things could turn around for me, and that's why I never gave up. I found out it's one thing to know the way, but it's another to actually go the way. Hope made me keep going toward the unfamiliar when it was easier to stay with the familiar. Hope sustained the woman when her health was killing her. And hope held me up when my brokenness was tearing me down. In the words of Jesse Jackson, "Keep hope alive!" Your breakthrough is up to you.

My prayer for you. *Father, I am so happy that You are omniscient. You know all things, about everything, and that includes every detail about each of us, and yet Your sacrificial love, grace, and forgiveness for us never ceases. Thank You that even though You know the path that we take, Your plan for our lives does not change. Thank You that all the good things and the issues in our lives are working together for our greater good. Thank You that knowing that helps to build our hope in You, and it encourages us to see our future better than where we are today. Thank You that there is no issue or problem in our life that is too hard for You to handle. I pray now that You will open the eyes of the women reading this book so that they see victory on the horizon instead of defeat. I pray that they embrace Your Word so that it builds hope and new vision. Now, Father, I thank You for Your vision for us and that Your eyes are always upon us. I thank You for what You've already done for each of us—I thank You that in spite of what it looks like, and in spite of what it feels like, we are victorious, and with hope and determination, we continue this journey to break through. In Jesus's name, amen.*

REFLECTION: IF IT AIN'T ONE THING, IT'S ANOTHER

You are well on your way through your journey to get your break-through. Do you see that this is not about putting blame on anyone? This is about identifying how your issue has affected your life and then coming to see that your real identity is not in what happened to you.

In which area has your issue affected your life? What problems has it caused? Physically? Mentally or emotionally? Financially? Spiritually? Relationally? Other?

1. How has your issue affected your identity? How do you see yourself? What does God say about you? (Read Jeremiah 29:11.) Regardless of the issues you may be experiencing, your life still matters to God. You are not what has happened to you; instead, you are who God says you are. You are not an accident or a mistake. God literally created you on purpose with a purpose, so start seeing yourself as you were created, not by what has happened, is happening, or will happen in your life.

2. Write down what the following scriptures say to you.
   - Romans 8:28: "And we know that God causes all things to work together for good to those who love God, to those who are called according to His purpose."
   - Deuteronomy 28:13: "If you pay attention to the commands of the Lord your God that I give you this day and carefully follow them, you will always be at the top, never at the bottom."

Start a vision board. On the left side of a piece of paper, write the heading "THIS IS ME NOW." On the right side, write the heading "MY FUTURE." Cut out pictures and words and glue them to the page so that they reflect your situation. Every day, look at your vision and read your scriptures and encouraging chants written throughout the book. Speak those things that are not as though they already are, and keep hope alive!

You are not what happened to you.
You are all God created you to be.

3

When Hope and Faith Collide

The woman with the issue of blood endured so much because of that one issue. She was sick, broke, and rejected. I imagine every time someone called her unclean, she was hurt to the bone. By now you've seen from my story the devastating effect of word wounds. How painful it must have been for this woman as well. For twelve years she had to identify herself as unclean. I sometimes wonder if she began to see herself by what others called her. Whoever said "sticks and stone may break my bones, but words will never hurt me" lied. Words hurt!

But all is not lost. There is a spark of hope in this story. In spite of what people called her, how they saw her, and how she may have even looked at herself, she never gave up trying to get her breakthrough. She had hope. Unfortunately, for twelve years, she had placed her hope in her money and in the doctors who failed her. But then something happened. The Bible said she heard about Jesus. I wondered how, when, and where did she go? The Levitical law forbid her to enter mainstream society, so did she just finally say, "It's all or nothing," and out of desperation go into the city and strike up a conversation with someone? Did she go sit with the crazy man who lived in the tombs (Mark 5:1–20)? Did she hear about Jesus healing the leper (Mark 1:40–42), who, like her, was considered unclean and was cast out of mainstream society? Did she somehow hear the stories of the prophets of old as they spoke of Jesus coming with healing in His wings. (Wings mean the hem/tassels on His robe, as in Malachi 4:2)? We don't know when, where, how, or exactly what she heard about Jesus. What we know is she already had hope that convinced her that her breakthrough *could* happen, but it was what she heard about Jesus that filled her with faith, and faith convinced her that her breakthrough *would* happen.

YOU NEED A PLAN

Against all odds, the doctors turning their heads and walking away, and what society said, and in spite of the danger she surely faced, she devised a plan that would take her right to her breakthrough. Now added to her hope and determination were a Word about Jesus, faith to believe and receive her breakthrough, and the plan to bring it to pass. Surely something good was going to happen!

DID YOU HEAR THAT? ARE YOU LISTENING?

I feel it is important to take a moment here before elaborating more about this woman and her faith to talk about hearing and listening. After reading her story several times, I became more cognizant of the importance of what we hear and listen to. Have you ever heard a poem, song, speech, sermon, or just a general conversation that literally rocked your world? I mean that after listening to it, you decided to do something that made a difference in your life, whether good or bad? The words we hear and listen to have power and are influential, whether negatively or positively. Can I just add this for free? I learned that lesson well through music. Although I love all kinds of music, ballads are my favorite. But more times than not, they got me in trouble a lot. Ballads put me in the mood for love— you know, candlelight dinners, hugging, kissing—yes, sex. Honey, I would premeditate committing fornication and adultery all because of a song I was listening to. Don't go judging me, because some of you are guilty of that too. But you get my point. I recognized music is a trigger for both good and bad responses, and now I am very mindful of who and what I listen to, and that especially means music.

When I read that the woman with the issue of blood heard something about Jesus that brought about such a powerful change in her life, I spent a lot of time trying to find out what she heard about Him. I wanted to know who said it because it is important what, and who you listen to. When people know you have issues and problems, they can mean well but their advice or counsel may not be what's right for your situation. Not only that, but even the news and social media give counsel or advice that is not always correct or appropriate. And to keep it real, so do many of our so-called Christian friends as well as leaders and politicians. Just because it is deemed politically correct doesn't mean it is morally, ethically, or biblically correct. Psalm 1, Proverbs 3:1–35, and many of the other scriptures found in Proverbs are crystal clear about the blessings of getting wise counsel. We also read about the outcomes of unwise counsel, and it is never good. What is key to this is that she didn't just hear the Word, but she listened to it, she believed it, she spoke it, and she acted on it. Yes, I believe there is a difference between hearing and listening. What you listen to can build you up or tear you down. It can build faith or fear. Keep reading.

Did you hear me? Are you listening to me? I bet you've heard that before. I would even go so far as to say you've said it a time or two to someone, especially children. I can still hear my grandma ask me those two questions after saying something to me. Most times I heard her voice, but I was too preoccupied with what I was doing to pay attention to what she said. I wasn't listening. Other times I heard her voice, I listened to what she said, but I simply disobeyed.

That always led to negative consequences. It was as a little girl that I learned through those experiences that there is a difference between hearing and listening. Thus, unless you are hearing impaired, you basically hear sound all the time, and I can prove that to you. As you've been reading this book, you've been hearing something: music, TV, voices in the background, a dishwasher, an air conditioner, the heater, the bus going down the street, and any number of things. But when you stop to listen, it takes on meaning. You mentally process the sound, you give it some thought, you reason it out, you make sense of it, and maybe you make a conscientious response to it—or not. Choose wisely what and who you listen to, for that determines how you make choices and decisions—good and bad. What you listen to can build up a positive sense of self-worth, hope, faith, and security. Or it can literally do just the opposite and tear you down to nothing. In this woman's story, listening to what was said about Jesus was her springboard to faith and ultimately to getting her breakthrough.

WATCH WHAT YOU SAY AND LISTEN TO

I am sure that many of you can relate to what I meant when I said that words hurt. I worked for several years with young men and women coming home from extended periods of incarceration. In our in-depth conversations, they would tell me things that someone had said to them when they were just little children that negatively affected their entire lives. Things like "You ain't nothing, ain't never gonna be nothing"; "You just like your ol' drunken father, and he ain't worth x!#%"; and "Look at ya, built like your mama; you gonna be a school dropout, single, having babies, just like her." Let me tell you something: these men and women wept, and often the men even sobbed as they spoke of the things their own parents or the ones they loved and trusted the most said to them and/or about them. The names they called them—stupid, bad, dumb, weak, fat, retard, ugly, and more—cut their little hearts like a knife. As adults, they still felt the blade every time someone spoke harshly to them or about them. Well into their adult lives, those words affected the decisions they made and those they allowed others to make concerning them. I'm telling you, words hurt! Grown men who had lived in the street, made it through drug-infested neighborhoods, spent time in solitary confinement in prison, and had been shot and stabbed multiple times, never whimpered, never frowned, never gave the slightest sign of discomfort as they spoke of those situations. And even when they did, they spoke of that pain as if they had simply stubbed their toe. None of the pain of the many experiences they spoke of could compare to the pain they experienced from spoken words.

As a little girl, I remember my grandparents telling me, "You are so smart. You can be an honor student, you can sing, you are pretty, you are friendly, and people like you." But I also remember hearing my mother say to me from the time I was a little girl to well into my young adult life that people didn't really like me. When I became a preteen and started to develop breasts and my butt began to round out, she told me the boys didn't really like me; they just wanted to "have sex with me." Unfortunately, when I listened to her say those things to me, it just further added to my low self-esteem. Consequently, I got into trouble a lot because I believed what she said and thought that in order to have girlfriends, I had to trade my clothes with them because my mom said the girls were jealous of my long hair and clothes. I lost many blouses like that, and I got in lots of trouble with my mom. When I stopped doing that, those girls I considered my closest friends were still around, but there was always that doubt in the back of my mind. Eventually I even cut my hair to a short Afro, believing to do so would mean I would fit in and people would like me. It was a long time before I accepted the fact that most people I associated with really did like me. I was generally a true and loyal friend, an encourager, and a kind and compassionate person. I just had this issue of needing to be chosen first.

I must admit that some of the guys in my circle of friends did want to play "touchy-feely" with me and more, but I found out that they were that way with most of the girls. To be honest, aside from some heavy kissing, they didn't press me for sex and respected me because I said no to having sex with them. My joy now is that several of those women and men are still my friends to this day. Still, my mom's voice kept ringing in my ears whenever someone would draw close to me. Consequently, for such a long time, I was suspicious of everyone and reluctant to get too emotionally attached to anyone for fear of being left or rejected. Those times when I was rejected or girlfriends or boyfriends didn't want to be my friends anymore floored me for months. It felt once again like abandonment and rejection, and I did not know how to appropriately process those feelings. For so long, it was easier for me to heal and get over a beating—I mean a serious whipping with black eyes and broken bones—than it was to get over the piercing to the core of the heart and soul by hurtful words spoken from one whom I trusted, admired, loved, and respected. Thus, my quest to be chosen first led me down the road of self-destruction for many years.

Watch what you say and listen to. Words have the power to condemn or confirm and to build faith or fear (Proverbs 18:21, 15:4, 11:9).

NOW FAITH IS...

It's important now to stop here to talk about faith a little more. Let's turn to the place where the word *faith* originated. The Bible explains faith in Romans 10:17 as coming from hearing the message, and the message is heard through the Word about Jesus. You can bank on it that God means what He says and says what He means. Whatever He says does not return to Him without having accomplished what He said it would do. Hebrews 11:1 says faith is the confidence that what we hope for will actually happen; you consider it done and act on it as if it already is. When we know and believe God's Word, it is then with both authority and assurance, like the woman with the issue of blood, that we can speak His Word, act on it, and see it come to pass. James 1:22 tells us that to have faith, we must do more than just hear the Word. For faith to be activated, we must listen, and we must do it (James 2:26). We literally live like what we've heard is true before it actually happens.

The woman with the issue of blood listened to the words that built her faith. Faith gave her the assurance she needed to pursue her breakthrough. In other words, she didn't just hear about Jesus and then go sit in a corner all sad and defeated. She listened, she believed, and she responded as she grabbed hold of that Word. Like one who chants over and over, she spoke those words that would lead her straight to her breakthrough: "If I can just touch the hem of His garment, I know I will be made whole."

It is from this portion of her story that I came to understand Proverbs 18:21, which tells us that life and death are in the power of the tongue. She exercised that power when she spoke of *breaking through* and not *breaking down* and literally started her journey to see those words come to pass. In other words, if you talk the talk, then you have got to walk the walk to see it manifest. She was a woman with an issue, but when she heard a Word about Jesus, faith was birthed, and she devised a plan. Yes, girlfriend, if you want a breakthrough, you need a Word about Jesus, the faith to believe it, and a plan to bring it to pass. I'm telling you, your breakthrough is up to you.

Around the beginning of 1987, I was still singing in clubs, getting high, and drinking every day and night, but it didn't have the same excitement for me anymore. You see, I'd begun to attend the concerts of a group of guys whom I used to sing with in the clubs. They had left the club scene and formed a Christian quartet band and singing group. The words of the songs they sang and the stories of how God had healed them physically and mentally, as well as their marriages, family relationships, and more, had such a profound effect on me. I didn't know it then, but as usual, God was working out His plan for my life. The more I hung out with them and listened to the words of the songs they sang, as well as their testimonies, the harder it became for me to go to the clubs and sing. All during the day, I began to sing those songs that spoke of God's forgiveness, healing power, amazing grace, and the love of Jesus for all mankind. At times I would wake myself up at night by literally singing those songs in my sleep. The words touched the very core of my being. I felt a longing, a need growing within me, to know more about Jesus. It was around this time that, from someplace deep inside me, I began to feel a breaking within; it was like I was being pulled away from the life I'd come so accustomed to living. I was listening, and I was believing and singing those songs. They convicted me while at the same time inspiring me and encouraging me to want to live better and to make wiser choices—the right choices. I started to search the Bible for the things the songs spoke of. Something was changing in me. I was listening, and I believed. My faith was increasing.

THINGS WILL GET BETTER

The Bible doesn't tell us how long it was from the time the woman with the issue of blood heard about Jesus and the time she got her breakthrough. But as you can see, my breakthrough began in increments of first breaking from within. I changed who and what I was listening to—people, music, TV—all of which influences what we believe and how we behave. I had to come to grips with the fact that there were certain men's voices that weakened me, so I stopped taking their calls, and when I'd run into them, my hello and good-bye were quick. Their voices were triggers for me, and I had to let them go completely.

The better my listening choices became, the easier it became for me to make wiser choices, to encourage myself (with or without the positive affirmations of others), and to see my situation as hopeful rather than as hopeless. I must admit I was still looking for outward change, but God was working on the inside. I still had the issues, but now I was beginning to identify them. I had no choice; God was exposing me to me. He was closing doors and opening doors, cutting people out of my life and bringing new people in.

On December 10, 1989, my life would take a turn from a place and space to which I would never return. I remember the night as if it happened yesterday. I was singing in a popular nightclub. I was high from snorting cocaine, and as usual, I had guzzled down several alcoholic drinks, but I didn't feel that regular high or drunk that I'd become so accustomed to. Somehow this time was different. I remember as I was putting the spoon of cocaine up to my nose, I was literally crying and saying out loud, "God, I don't want to do this anymore." Around midnight, I was standing on the stage singing. It was the last song of that set, and we were about to take a break. I can still see the setting. The club was filled to capacity. I was so high. I was holding on to that mic stand, singing my heart out, when out of nowhere, in the middle of the song, I heard someone say, "My child, you will do this no longer." Now mind you, I was really feeling and singing the song, but when I heard that voice, I looked around to see if the DJ was on the mic talking to me. I thought, "Maybe the song is not right for this atmosphere." But the DJ wasn't even in the booth. I kept singing, and I heard it a second time. I looked at all my band members, and they were all in their own personal groove, so I searched the audience with my eyes, but no one appeared to have spoken to me. I stopped singing so that it was just the instruments playing, and I heard it a third time, but it was more intense. As I listened, I knew I was hearing the voice of God. It was firm, yet I could feel the compassion. It drew me in, and it pulled me out. Suddenly, I did not want to be there in that club. I finished that song, gathered my personal belongings, left my drugs and my worldly music charts, and headed home, crying all the way. I knew my life was about to take a major turn. I didn't know how or why, but in my gut, I knew my life would never be the same. Another breaking had begun in me.

In that thirty-minute drive home, I kept crying out, "God, please help me. I don't want to live like this anymore." By the time I walked in my door, I was physically sick. I remember so vividly taking a shower and then lying on the floor beside my bed. What I know now is that while I was washing the outside, God was doing a heavy-duty washing and cleaning of my heart and my mind. As I lay on that floor, sick, scared, and in humble surrender, I cried out to God that I had had enough. I promised God that morning that if He would deliver me, then I would stop singing in clubs and bars, and I would do like the guys with the Gospel group: I would sing for Him. That was my plan. But you know God's plan for me would take me far beyond just that.

When I woke up later that day, I knew—I knew with every ounce of my being—that my cocaine and alcohol addictions and that club lifestyle would no longer be a part of my life. I was not only sober but also knew that God had delivered me from those addictions. I didn't know anything about rehab and NA/AA twelve-step programs at that time. Hear this: God is the healer, and He is the deliverer. What I know is when I began to follow those Gospel groups, and when I began to sing those sweet Gospel songs, I believed the words. I sang, "Amazing grace, how sweet the sound that saved a wretch like me. I once was lost but now I'm found, was blind but now I see." I didn't even know what a wretch was, I just knew it was me. I declare to you today without hesitation that it was God's amazing grace that saved me. God did it for me, and He will do it for you. God was breaking me out, but my breakthrough had not yet come.

Immediately after that, I became very sick, and I was in and out of the doctor's office and the hospital, but no one could tell me what was wrong. I realized that not only was God breaking me and purifying my heart and my thinking but also He was literally purging my body of the drugs and drink and residue of the promiscuous life He'd delivered me from. As I was spiritually healing, growing, and maturing, my physical health was getting better as well. It was during this time that I began to write songs and produce music that would result in my first full solo album, called Restore My Faith. *I told you God's plan would be greater than the one I had for myself. I planned on just going back to church and joining the choir (I did) and singing solos, as well as at weddings and funerals (I did), but God's plan was bigger. That CD afforded me the opportunity to travel throughout the country and to several of the Caribbean Islands to share my story and to minister in song. I was interviewed on local and national radio stations and never failed to tell my story and to give God the glory. It opened the door for me to start singing and speaking in churches and to sing on programs with some world-renowned singers and musicians.*

With a Word, a song, and a heart full of faith, I wanted to be free from my troubled and hurtful past. It had been a long journey for me. I knew deep within my heart that an even greater change was coming. I didn't know how or when, but I knew somehow I was going to get my breakthrough.

For such a long time, I felt my life was worth nothing to anyone. I was lost, without direction and purpose. It got to the point where I stopped loving myself, and I just went through the motions of surviving. I went from man to man, seeking validation, love, and to be chosen first, only to find myself feeling more alone, worthless, and hurting more than ever. I felt my family only tolerated me, and I sought refuge with strangers, drugs, alcohol, and sex. I considered myself a friend to so many, but I really had only a few true friends. I thought I would die before I was thirty, and when I turned thirty, I couldn't see myself past thirty-five. But let me tell you that God is so faithful. Absolutely nothing was going to stop His plan for my life. Oh, did I mention that, at this very moment that I am writing this, I am sixty-five years old? I don't look like what I have been through, and I have no diseases that are normally attached to someone who has lived the life I have. Oh yes, I found out that God is faithful to do just what His Word says. God's Word, the promises we read in the Bible, don't change because of our nonbelief and behavior. But they are activated in our life by our belief/faith and behavior.

BREAKING DOWN BEFORE THE BREAKTHROUGH

Some would say right here, "OK, you got your breakthrough. Now what?" But let me caution you: I was breaking within. My ways of seeing things, my thinking, and my processing of situations was different. I was breaking down and letting go of bad habits, bad relationships, and bad thoughts and ideologies. I learned I had to change people, places, things, and situations. And I was getting some breaks along the way. New doors were opening—better opportunities, the right opportunities—but this was by no means my breakthrough. You see, when I looked at the woman with the issue of blood and the path she took to get her breakthrough, it brought validity to one of the meanings of the word *breakthrough*. It is a military term meaning a sudden forward thrust through *and* beyond the enemy's line of defense. So as good as it was for me, this was not my breakthrough. God was simply preparing me, breaking me down, and bringing me to a place of humble submission to His Word, His ways, His will, and His plans for my life (1 Peter 5:6). I still had a ways to go. God's plan for me was greater than merely not going to the clubs, no longer getting high and drunk, and changing the genre of the music I was singing. And I believe it was no different for the woman with the issue of blood because her plan was to touch Jesus, be healed in her body, and go on about her business. But God had a greater plan for her as well. And I believe His plan for you is greater than what you may have planned for yourself.

SPEAK NOW

Quick review. For the woman with the issue of blood, her journey to her breakthrough began when she heard about Jesus. She got a

Word, she listened, she believed, she came up with a plan, and she began to speak to herself. Her words reminded her constantly that her healing was inevitable. It was just a matter of time.

You have got to start now—today—and speak life over your situation. Speak victory, not defeat. Remove the word *can't* from your vocabulary. I declare to you this day that you can do all things through Christ who strengthens you (Philippians 4:13). I don't care if you don't believe it yet. You keep speaking it till it gets down inside your belly, till you go to sleep saying it, till you wake up saying it. Say it throughout the day. Write it down on paper and post it on your refrigerator, your closet doors, your front and back doors, and the mirrors in your house. Put your picture beside it. If you have an automobile, put it on your steering wheel and on the dashboard. Put it on your desk. This goes for you in the shelter, you in the prison, you living under the bridge. Read it out loud, over and over again. Get it down inside you. Put melody to it, and sing it if you have to, but speak God's Word, speak His promises, speak life, and speak victory over and over.

My special prayer for you. *God, I pray that at this point You send a Word to the one reading this book and that she may not just hear the Word but believe the Word, speak it, and act on it. I pray You remove those people, places, things, and situations out of her way that would hinder her journey to her breakthrough. Give her the holy boldness to repeat Your Word openly and without guilt, shame, or fear. I pray You make manifest every promise of Yours that she believes in her heart and speaks out of her mouth. Release her fears and open her eyes and ears so that she can discern the times and seasons and act accordingly. Place a plan down in her spirit that supersedes anything she could ever ask or think, and give her the will to act on it. Thank You that You are able to do exceedingly, abundantly above all we could ever ask or think. I believe You are able to save the life, heal the body, restore the mind and the broken relationships, and provide all the needs of* *the one reading this book. Now, Father, wipe away the tears, heal all the hurts in her heart, and remove all doubt. Be strong in the weak, and get all the honor and glory and praise, for it is by Your hand and Your grace alone that we have come this far and can move forward to our breakthrough.*

REFLECTION: WHEN HOPE AND FAITH COLLIDE

It is not enough to just hear something. You must learn to listen and to choose wisely who you listen to. Listening means paying attention to what is being said, processing it, and subsequently acting on it in one way or another. Faith requires listening to God's Word, believing, and acting on it (speaking). Read and answer the following questions.

1. What were you *hoping* could happen in your life, but now that you have faith, you believe and live like you *know* it will happen?

2. Who and what do you spend most of your time listening to?
   - Who is your confidant?
   - Who is the person(s) you go to for advice?

3. What kind of music are you listening to? What songs are you singing?
   - What do the lyrics say?
   - Does the music activate faith, fear, lust, learning, and so on?

4. What have you heard and believe about Jesus?
   - What are you going to do about it?

Positive affirmations and scriptures to repeat to yourself:

- Psalm 30:2: "O God I cried out to you and you healed me."
- Psalm 147:3: "God heals the brokenhearted and binds up their wounds."
- Psalm 139:13–18: "I am not an accident or a mistake."
- Romans 8:37: "My victory will go beyond what I ever imagined."

Faith will work if you work it.

4

You're on the Right Road Now

Wow, what stories, huh? The woman with the issue of blood was sick, broke/destitute, desperate, and cast out of mainstream society. However, when she heard about Jesus, her faith was ignited, and she began her journey to her breakthrough. Once again, remember now, the Bible is not very explicit about her journey. We read only of her destination. But if you will allow me again the opportunity to use my imagination coupled with the history of the text, I'll tell you what I believe might have happened that day.

The King James Bible says that a thronging crowd followed Jesus (Mark 5:24). Perhaps you've experienced a thronging crowd during an athletic event, concert, or church event. The crowd is so thick that people are literally breast to back and toe to heel. Well, Jesus was always either in the midst of or being followed by that kind of crowd. In order to touch Jesus, this woman, regarded as unclean, had to maneuver her way through this crowd to anonymously make contact with Him. Interestingly, she wasn't the only sick person in the crowd. In my research, I discovered that the crowds were most often filled with people seeking healing and deliverance from various sicknesses/diseases and situations. She had to press through that and more. The crowd also consisted of those who rejected and mocked Jesus. The Scribes and Pharisees were often in there, but they didn't believe Jesus was Christ and sought to catch Him in a lie to try to prove He was an imposter. The disciples were there, but Thomas was a doubter, Peter was a denier, and the others would soon abandon Jesus. Still others in the crowd, oppressed and sick, wanted and needed healing or a breakthrough, but from this story, it seemed they did not have the courage or faith to believe they would get it.

Nevertheless, this woman, at the risk of being discovered and maybe put to death, decided to get in the crowd to touch the hem of Jesus's garment. I used to believe like so many that she crawled through that crowd to get to Jesus, but there is no way she could have been crawling around on the ground in this type of crowd. It's possible that she was bent over, but not on her knees, at least not yet. To do so would surely mean being trampled, maimed, or killed. But with determination now fueled by faith overriding her fear, she got in that crowd. She no longer heard what people called her or cared about the doctor's bad report. She wasn't concerned anymore with who left her or who hurt her, but rather, her focus was on her mission to touch Jesus. All she heard was her own encouraging voice speaking over and over again what she believed about Jesus. Little did she know that that crowd was the road to her breakthrough.

WHAT'S IN YOUR CROWD?

As I began to think more about the fact that she had to go through that thronging crowd to get her breakthrough, it reinforced my belief that we all have our own crowd. I call it the crowd of opposition. This is merely those hindrances—the people, places, things, thoughts, emotions, and situations—that get in your way. They go before you and cause you to take detours or paths not aligned with getting your breakthrough. Things like anger, fear, unforgiveness, resentment, and bitterness cloud your vision, stymie your walk, and ultimately block your way. Fear will raise its nasty head and have you scared of being victorious, scared of actually getting your break-through, because you think as soon as it happens, something bad will happen, or you will mess up or fail. So every time something good happens, you do or say something to sabotage it. But I am here to tell you that fear is just a trick of the devil. God did not give us the spirit of fear. God has given us a holy boldness and the right way to think (2 Timothy 1:7). Let's take a closer look at this thronging crowd.

ENVY AND JEALOUSY

For some envy and jealousy are in the crowd, pulling at your heart and mind as they constantly remind you that others around you are succeeding, healthy, married, and have great jobs, homes, hus-bands, and more. It hinders your progression as you become so focused on comparing yourself with others or wanting what others have. Envy and jealousy left alone to fester will cause you some major mental, emotional, and yes, financial and physical damage, as they are the breeding ground of bitterness, resentment, and hostility. Eventually you lose focus on your own self-worth, good-ness, victories, and journey as your hope is steadily depleted and your self-esteem diminishes. Envy has the potential to cause you to lose faith and to stop believing in yourself and God. You must know you are valuable to God, even in your worst moments. Press through envy and jealousy.

PRIDE

The woman with the issue of blood had to deal with pride. Her is-sue overshadowed who she was and robbed her of her identity. She was spoken of by her issue and not by her name. People called her unclean. But that did not stop her. She just kept repeating over and over again, "If I can just touch the hem of His garment, I know I'll be made whole." Those words were the fire of faith burning in her and the key to her progression. Her focus was on her breakthrough. She moved with the crowd, and you must do the same.

Pride was a part of my crowd. If I were a gambling woman, I would bet that it's in your crowd as well. It was so difficult for me because I had to deal with the negative things that people who knew me said to me and about me, as well as what those who did not know me or have a clue about what my issues were said to me and about me. I was ashamed of how I had been living and of a lot of the decisions I made. It humbled me. In order to get my breakthrough, I had to keep my head up but not in a cocky way. I had to walk with the confidence that what I heard about Jesus and God's Word was greater than what others said to me or about me.

God's Word about us is greater than shame and our pride. Please get a grip on this: the Bible says we are fearfully and wonderfully made by God on purpose, with purpose, power, provision, and His promises for our life. These promises belong to all who will believe (Psalm 139:13–17; Jeremiah 1:5, 29:11). Don't you know that God even knows the number of the hairs on our heads (Matthew 10:30)? He knows our thoughts before we think them and what we'll do before we do it (Psalm 139:1–4). Yet it does not cancel out His purpose for our life. No matter the bad decisions or the horrible things we did or said or that were done or said to and about us, none of these things cancels out God's purpose and plans for our life. I am and you are just who God says we are. Absolutely nothing changes that.

TRADITION AND LEGALISM

I think the woman with the issue of blood had to deal with tradition and legalism. Back then a single woman had no business being out in that crowd of men, dignitaries, Scribes and Pharisees, disciples, and Jesus. That didn't matter to her that day. Touching Jesus was more important to her than the traditions of man. Coupled with tradition was legalism: her issue of blood meant she was not supposed to be in the general public areas, much less in the crowd, brushing up against anything or anybody. Bottom line, according to the traditions and legalism of her time, she had no business being in that crowd. But it did not stop her.

I also had to deal with tradition. You see, in part, getting my break-through would mean answering my call to preach. That was so hard for me because the people I loved and trusted the most with my life, my dreams, and my aspirations were my immediate family, but in so many ways, their beliefs in the roles of women were tied to traditions. They simply did not believe it was appropriate for women to be preachers. Tradition in my family said women were either housewives or government employees who got married, had babies, took care of their husbands, children, and homes and went to church and served as an usher or nurse or sang in the choir. Don't get me wrong, I am not saying there is something wrong with that. To each his own. But you know by now that was not my calling, and that certainly is not my story.

DOUBT

There is still more in the crowd of opposition, and I believe this one has the potential to make you turn around just steps away from your breakthrough. I am talking about doubt. Doubt is a dream killer and a faith slayer. It walks beside you to speak negativity into your ears to rob you of your hope, make you forget your dream, and endeavor for you to lose your faith and determination. You can have all the tools in your hand, all the money you need, and more, but doubt will have you saying to yourself, "I can't do this, I don't have the right tools or education, I don't have enough money, I'm not smart enough," and more. And although all that may be true, I am reminded that the Bible says, "We can do all things through Christ who strengthens us" (Philippians 4:13). If we have cares and burdens, we can entrust them to God in confession, meditation, and prayer and know that

He will handle it according to His promises, His will, and His way regarding our situation (Matthew 11:28). Don't doubt. Believe God. Have faith.

Doubt beat me up bad. I did not have a college degree. I certainly didn't have any bank accounts, and at times, I barely had enough money to pay my monthly bills. Although I always looked good, my clothes came from thrift stores. I learned to cut and style my own hair and nails, and no one knew the difference. Still, I compared myself to those who shopped at high-end stores and wore designer clothes and shoes.

I was full of self-doubt. I was invited to sing on stage to open for some of the world's greatest Christian and secular singers and groups, but doubt about my singing gift would literally make me sick just before a performance. I was so intimidated by the gifts and talents of others. But God would send a message and a messenger to help me break free from the opposition of doubt. I remember the day so vividly: I had to sing at the funeral of one of my best friends. On the program to sing before me was a world-renowned male vocalist. My stomach churned, and I dreaded my time to get up to sing after him. Doubt about my own abilities tore into my gut and opened the door for fear to kick in. I was a nervous wreck. But I had to sing. As always, God used what He put in me to bring glory to His name. And, as always, after I sang, I was so ashamed of myself for doubting the gift that God has given me.

If you're dealing with doubt, please get this. I leaned several lessons that day that I must still call on from time to time. First, our gifts are not about us, and whenever we are called upon to use our gifts, we must first go to God in prayer and submit to Him our will, our way, and our desire to draw any attention to our gifts or ourselves. When we submit to God like that, trust Him, and seek to bring glory and honor to Him and not us or our gift(s), I promise you, He uses us mightily. The second lesson came that same day from the mouth of my pastor after the funeral was over. He had observed my response when the people clapped and shouted for the star performer who sang before me, and then he observed my defeated stance when it was my time to sing. He later told me, "Nikki, you don't ever have to feel bad or be intimidated by anybody else's singing ability. You may not have the world's greatest voice, but there is something rare and unique about your voice that touches the hearts of people. You have God's anointing. And that gives you power. People clapped and shouted after you sang just like they did for that entertainer who just sang, but there was a difference. The difference was while we enjoyed hearing you sing, and we always do, we clapped and shouted unto God. Your anointed singing brings us into the presence of God, and people get healed and delivered, and they open their hearts to God. Then He gets the honor, He gets the praise, and He gets the glory that belongs only to Him."

I learned that the glory was not about me. It never has been, and it never will be. It's all about God getting the glory from our lives and using us to draw others unto Him. And often, God will use the least likely, the forgotten, and the unknown to bring about the biggest impact. I decided that day to keep moving with the crowd. Don't compare yourself to others. Don't let doubt stop you. You can do this. Move with the crowd.

LIES

Still, there is opposition in the crowd that will literally shut you down just steps away from your breakthrough. I'm speaking of lies. Lies tell you that you'll never get your breakthrough, no matter what you do. Lies will convince you that you are a failure, that you've done too much to be forgiven by God and people. Lies will tell you that this is just life, that this is all there is and to just get used to it. Lies will tell you there is no God, that the Bible is man's word to control people's lives. Lies say Jesus may have existed, but He's just a man like any other man. Lies will knock the wind out of you and will throw a nonbeliever or one with little faith off the path quickly. But I can tell you firsthand that people never, ever have the last say over and about our life. God does. I cried out to God many times for many different things, and even though He may not have revealed the answer when and the way I wanted, in the long run, He did answer, and His answer has always been the best thing for me. I also learned that our life is not just about us. What happens to us, the things we do and say—good, bad, or otherwise—somehow have an effect on those in our circle of family, friends, acquaintances, and those we meet along the way, which often means for generations to come.

Lies will tell us we have no future. But I found out that what we see is the "right now" in our situations, and that might not look or feel good. But God knows our future. He knows the end from the beginning (Isaiah 46:10). Now ain't that good news! I learned that whether or not you believe in Him and whether or not you believe the Word, it does not make Him any less real or the Word of no influence. God is God. Jesus is the Lord, and His Word is truth, whether you believe it or not. I challenge you to try Him and to see that the Lord is good.

I learned that nothing happens that God is not aware of, and that there is a purpose in everything, even if we don't know it or understand why. Can I tell you I am still learning to trust the process as I pursue my purpose? Our ways are not God's ways. We must trust that somehow it is all working together for His glory and our good. Don't let lies discourage, disappoint, and ultimately keep you from getting your breakthrough. Believe God. Trust God's Word. Speak His promises over your life. His Word won't fail you. Keep moving with the crowd.

AFFAIRS OF THE HEART AND FINANCES
Then there are the affairs of the heart and finances: your loved one dies, your husband cheats, your daughter gets pregnant at thirteen

years old, your son is locked up again, your parent is diagnosed with a life-threatening disease, your car is repossessed, your job is lost, your home is foreclosed on, you're homeless. These situations and more have the potential to throw you into long periods of grief, harden your heart, and stifle your emotions and your will to go on. You must stay focused. Remember why you are there in the first place, and speak God's Words of affirmation, peace, and healing over and over until they do just what they say. The woman with the issue of blood was alone, sick, and broke, but she kept going. Don't ever forget that God is our provider, the source of everything we need and could ever want (Philippians 4:19). You keep going.

Please know that all the trouble and all the heartache are just a part of the process. Learn from your pain, grow through your pain, trust the process, and get your breakthrough. Contrary to how it feels, this is not the end. God is the mender of the brokenhearted (Psalm 147:3). Keep moving with the crowd.

FRIENDS AND FAMILY

By now you probably know that everybody with you is not for you. The crowd of opposition consists of people who walk with you (to a point), but they don't believe for one minute that you'll get your breakthrough. They are just along for the ride, waiting with the same bait dangling in your face that has kept you in bondage all along—misery does love company. There are those who will be there to encourage you but only from a distance because they have their own set of issues and are mainly focused on how to get their own breakthroughs.

There were very few people who believed in me and who supported my journey for change. The offers of drugs and alcohol came often, but I said no. Club singing engagements that I had wanted for so long were finally offered to me, but I said no. I had to remember my triggers and to just say no to those things that could and would draw me back down the path God was delivering me from. The Bible says in Hebrews 12:1 that we are to put away the things that will hinder us in reaching our destination. Stay focused. You're almost there.

I admit I thought I had made it through my crowd that night in 1989 when I broke free of the drugs, alcohol, and club lifestyle. I also thought I got my breakthrough when I began singing with the Christian band and in the church choir. But that wasn't so. You see, even though drinking, clubbing, and drugging were major problems, they were not my issue. Abandonment, rejection, a lack of positive self-esteem, and a desire to be chosen first were my issues, and they still had me in their grip. Drugs, alcohol, and the club lifestyle had been my medications to numb me from the pain of my past and the issues it caused. Truth be told, I ended up substituting the drugs, alcohol, and club life with something else. Oh, it's true that I could sing and shout all day and night and bring the fire of God down in a church service or concert hall. There was always a crowd of people around me afterward. But I wasn't seeking fame, fortune, and the applause of a crowd. I still wanted to be chosen first, so I'd still end up in competition for somebody's love, affection, and attention. Consequently, I was in and out of relationships and affairs that led nowhere. Sex became my drug and drink, and I guess you could say church became my nightclub. After all, some of the men and women I had sung and danced with in the clubs I also sang and danced with in the church. It was just a different venue, a different dance, and different music. (Don't judge me; learn from me.)

GUILT

The Bible says the crowd is thronging; it is thick, and it is tight. I discovered there is opposition in the crowd that comes up from behind to remind you of your past and to make you feel unworthy of a breakthrough. Yes, I am speaking of guilt. Guilt keeps us chained behind the bars of our mind. It constantly reminds us of our mistakes:

unwed mother, history of incarceration, active sex life and now living with HIV/AIDS or some other communicable disease, losing your kids, abortions, divorce, sexual perversions, adultery, cheating on taxes, and so much more.

As I was going through my crowd of opposition, guilt came riding in on the coattails of my low self-esteem and need to be first. I met him at church where we both were members. It was nothing beyond the church hello and comments about the service. He was married with children—a hardworking man. Nothing about the way he looked, dressed, or behaved was what I was generally attracted to in any regard. I never thought for one moment about having any kind of relationship with him. He just wasn't my type. One day he overheard me say that I needed some work done in my home, and he volunteered to help me out at a minimal cost. (You already know, don't you, that eventually that would be a big price for me to pay.)

We began to talk a lot about our Christian beliefs, the church, and our individual life stories. I was so comfortable talking with him. He was the first man whom I told my real story to—all of it—and he listened without judgment. That's when he began to tell me about some of the issues he had and his troubled marriage (the devil was setting this thing up). He began to help me out when I had concerts. He would come to my home and load up his truck with boxes of albums, cassette tapes, and sound equipment. Often he would bring his little daughter with him. We laughed when people used to make comments about us being a good-looking family, but it didn't mean anything to me at first.

Unfortunately, over time, I came to love that feeling of support and family, even if it was a lie. He became my confidant, my best friend. But then something happened. He began to choose spending time with me rather than being home with his wife. I had no intentions of letting it get to that point, and I really don't believe that he did either, but after two years, by the time I realized what was happening, we were so emotionally attached that becoming intimate with him seemed so natural. You already know my issue of wanting to be chosen first. Well, the idea that he chose me first gave me a false sense of importance and security. I knew it was wrong, but it felt like it filled a void I suffered with for thirty years.

We both knew it had to end, and finally, he told me he was going back home to his wife and kids. The one who had chosen me first was now leaving me for the one he had chosen me over. I was never really first. I felt like I did the day my daddy walked out of my life and my mommy sent me to live with my grandparents. The tragedy in this story is that he died unexpectedly not long after our breakup. Consequently, on top of grieving the loss of our relationship and the devastating news of his death, our affair became public knowledge, which brought with it guilt and shame and more pain than I could ever imagine. Once again, I spiraled down into a depression so deep that death really seemed to be my only solace. My depression was long and hard. I lost my job and my apartment, and I almost lost my mind. I convinced myself that nobody would or should ever really love me, and that God certainly didn't love me either, especially after that.

I had the opportunity a year or so after he died to meet with his wife and daughter to apologize and to ask for forgiveness. When I walked away, I felt some of the heaviness of hurting them drop from my heart, but the disappointment in myself, as well as the guilt and shame, haunted me for years.

For those of you wondering if I went back to using drugs and alcohol, the answer is no. I told you God had delivered me from those demons, and it's true that when God sets you free, you are free indeed (John 8:36). It's sealed. Still, I was a mess. One day, a dear friend of mine who knew all about it ministered to me with a scripture that started me back on my journey to my breakthrough. John 1:9 says that if we confess our sins to God, then God is faithful in that He will forgive us of our sins and remove the guilt. I broke free from the guilt and shame of that relationship, and I can tell you that was the last time I would ever have another affair. That was 1995.

I am a living witness that God will forgive you, and He will give you another chance if you seek Him earnestly, with your whole heart and mind. He will take away the guilt and shame and fill you with humility, joy, and peace because His faithfulness to do just what His Word promises is everlasting. Keep moving with the crowd.

I hope you haven't taken the position of judge and jury over my life at this point. We all have a past; none of us is perfect. And let's be clear: Wrong is wrong. Sin is sin.

I imagine if you can really be honest here, if you are on your journey to getting your breakthrough, you probably could relate to some of what I've shared with you in this chapter. Many of you, I'm sure, have so much more opposition than I could write in this book. But I shared all that with you so you can see that nothing can stop you from getting your breakthrough unless you allow it. Take your eyes off the opposition, stay focused on your destiny, and by all means, keep moving with the crowd. Your breakthrough is up to you.

BREAKING FREE TO BREAK THROUGH

I realized after all that that I was far from getting my breakthrough. Let me remind you of the meaning of breakthrough. Wiktionary defines breakthrough as "advancing through and past enemy lines." That's the kind of breakthrough I am talking about. That's the kind of breakthrough the woman with the issue of blood got. Her plan was to just touch Jesus, to be healed in her body, and to go about her business. But God had a greater plan for her. He has a greater plan for me, and He has a greater plan for you. Keep reading, and keep moving with the crowd.

GETTING THROUGH THE CROWD

The crowd of opposition is something to be reckoned with, isn't it? How can you go through the crowd to get your breakthrough? How could that woman with the issue of blood do it? She had to have been so weak and so frail. Why would she go through the shame, pain, and possible humiliation? At one point, I asked those same questions. I mean, at least she had been living with that issue for twelve years. She was handling it. But the fact is she never settled for it, and don't you settle either.

So many people and situations were in her way, blocking and hindering her. Isn't it the same for you? How did she manage to get to Jesus to get her breakthrough? How can you? How did I? I remember an experience I had once with a thronging crowd, and now I know the lesson I learned in the crowd that day had nothing to do with the physical crowd, but God showed me something that I would need as I sought a breakthrough in my life and would one day share with others how to do the same.

FOCUS AND FORTITUDE

I was attempting to leave a large concert stadium that seated over eighteen thousand. That night the stadium was filled to capacity. When I stepped out of the arena area into the main hall, the crowd of people was literally thick like packed sardines and moved at a snail's pace. I am barely five feet tall, so all I could see was the middle of most people's backs. Instinctively, I suppose, I looked forward and up toward the ceiling, and there, not too far ahead, was that blessed red light that said, "EXIT." But there were just too many people in the hall for me, so I figured I'd just go back into the arena area and wait a few moments for the crowd to get smaller, but I couldn't move. I am claustrophobic, so my mind was telling me that there was no way I was going to make it in that crowd at that slow pace. Consequently, I started pushing and yelling, "Coming out," as I tried to get across to the opposite side of that great hall and crowd to the wall on the same side as the exit sign. That was a horrible mistake. I was cursed at, cursed out, and pushed until I was right in the middle, farther away from the wall on either side. Even though I was in the middle of the crowd, they had pushed me forward.

Needless to say, I was now terrified. To keep fear from paralyzing me and to keep myself from going into a panic, I looked back up and focused on that exit light. Somehow, through all that noise coming from the crowd, I heard, "Stay focused on the light. Everybody's heading toward the light. Move with the crowd." I was scared, and like the old saying goes, when the pain of staying the same is finally greater than the pain of change, you will do something different. I became more determined, more focused on getting unstuck. I focused on the exit sign, and I kept saying to myself over and over, "Nikki, just stay focused on the light. Everybody's heading toward the light. Move with the crowd." And I did until I looked up, and I was walking under that light and into the parking lot. I declare to you, the very situation that could have brought me harm and the very things that were boxing me in were actually the catalyst for me getting out of that hall and into the parking lot.

Do you get it? I learned some good lessons in that crowd and from reading this woman's story. Sometimes the very things that get in the way of our breakthrough are the very things God uses to push us to our breakthrough. Sickness, divorce, unemployment, grief, homelessness, betrayal, and all the other things I have written about and so much more will push you to pray and cry until you get your breakthrough. I learned that delayed breakthrough does not mean denied breakthrough. Opposition can hurt me, it certainly can hinder me, but it will no longer stop me. All I'm saying here is don't let the crowd of opposition stop you; instead, let it push you to your breakthrough.

FAITH, FOCUS, AND FORTITUDE

Regardless of the opposition in that crowd following Jesus, the woman with the issue of blood didn't give up. Pride didn't stop her.

Tradition and worldly legalism didn't stop her. She never allowed her fear to paralyze her. She was not guided by her emotions, but rather, her fortitude was based on what she heard, believed, and ultimately spoke about Jesus. It was faith. Faith kept her moving through the crowd when fear said to turn and run. Faith kept her moving when doubt said it'll never happen. Faith became her strength to walk when her physical body had long since lost its natural ability. She never lost her focus, and she never lost sight of her goal—to touch the hem of Jesus's garment and to get her breakthrough.

Getting my breakthrough was a faith walk for me as well. Yes, even when it didn't look like my breakthrough was going to happen, and especially when it did not feel like it was going to happen, I held on to what I heard and believed and sang about Jesus. I held on to God's Word. Ultimately, I learned that faith is not based on feelings. Faith is based on facts, and those facts are God's Word and that Jesus is everything the Bible says, and Jesus can do whatever the Bible says He can do. That is what you must believe; that is what you speak, sing, pray, meditate on; and that is what you must act on. Faith built on the facts will propel you to your breakthrough.

A special prayer for you. *God, I pray that at this point my readers have come to their crowds of opposition with faith, focus, and fortitude based on your Word regarding their situations. I pray that You are revealing to my readers all they need to confront their issues, and that at the same time, You are empowering them to keep moving in spite of the crowd of opposition so that they may complete this journey victoriously. Open their eyes that they might see Your guiding light; open their arms that they might embrace Your unconditional love, grace, and mercy; and open their ears that they might hear Your words of instruction. And God, please open their hearts to forgive those who hurt, abandoned, rejected, and lied to them so that You may in turn forgive them and free their hearts and minds to move to their breakthroughs. God, when they can't see Your hand at work in their lives,* *please show them Your heart as you take away the guilt and shame of their past, as well as the fear that has held them hostage for so long, and create in them all a clean heart. Oh God, renew the right spirit within them. In Jesus's name, amen.*

REFLECTION: WHAT'S IN YOUR CROWD?

Exercise. On a piece of paper, draw a large circle that almost takes up the entire page. In the middle of the circle, put a small red circle and fill it in with red. Next, draw multiple circles inside the larger circle until there is no more room to do so. The circles represent the thronging crowd in your life. The center represents the place of breakthrough. Your assignment is to write the words in the lines of your circles that represent the opposition in your crowd. You must be very honest, because at this point, the crowd should be all that's standing between you and your breakthrough. Your breakthrough is on the way.

1. Read the following scriptures, and write down what they are saying to you.
   - Psalm 27:1-3: "The Lord is my light and my salvation— whom shall I fear? The Lord is the stronghold of my life—of whom shall I be afraid? When the wicked advance against me to devour me, it is my enemies and my foes who will stumble and fall. Though an army besiege me, my heart will not fear; though war break out against me, even then I will be confident."
   - Psalm 118:5-6: "I called upon the Lord in distress: the Lord answered me, and set me in a large place. The Lord is on my side; I will not fear: what can man do unto me?"
   - 2 Corinthians 4:16-18: "Therefore we do not lose heart. Though outwardly we are wasting away, yet inwardly we are being renewed day by day. For our light and momentary troubles are achieving for us an eternal glory that far outweighs them all. So we fix our eyes not on what is seen, but on what is unseen, since what is seen is temporary, but what is unseen is eternal."

If you want something different,
you've got to do something different.

The Last Mile of the Way

She can hardly hear herself speak for the roar of the crowd...all those people: some lame, some blind, some deaf. There are married, separated, divorced, and single people. There are mansion owners and shelter dwellers. There are CEOs and the unemployed. There are rich, and there are poor. There are teachers and students, preachers and pastors. There are pimps and business owners. There are drug dealers, doctors, bankers, thieves, prostitutes, addicts, abusers, abused, offenders, and offended. There are the world renowned, and there are the last, the least, and the forgotten; men and women, boys and girls, all in the crowd following Jesus. How will she ever get to touch the hem of His garment?

She won't be able to keep the pace much longer...the pushing and shoving and bumping up against one another has made her already aching, feeble body now spasm with pain...fear and the thought of death still loom heavily as she remembers that she is unclean, that she shouldn't be in that crowd....but all she needs is a touch. If she can just touch the hem of His garment...she moves with the crowd...

What's happening? Why is the crowd getting nosier? Why are they pushing so hard? Wait a minute...suddenly, without warning, without time to think about it, without time to get into a pivotal position, there, straight ahead of her...the wings on his robe; those blue-and-white tassels, just like the prophets said. She reaches...she chants, "If I can just touch the hem of His garment."

Do it—do it now. Grab it now. It takes her breath away.

But the woman, fearing and trembling, aware of what had happened to her, came and fell down before Him and told Him the whole truth. And He said to her, "Daughter, your faith has made you well; go in peace, and be healed of your issue." *Mark 5:33–34*

5

The Last Mile of the Way

What a journey for the woman with the issue of blood. So much was going against her for those twelve years. Then on top of all the problems her issue caused, she had to deal with that thronging crowd too! That alone is enough to discourage anybody. But in spite of it all, she did not give up. And since you're still reading this, I pray that it means you have not given up either. It is of no matter if you are stumbling or falling along the way. I don't care how long it has taken you to read this book or to get to this place in your journey. The most important thing is that you are still in the crowd, you are still on your way to your breakthrough. I'm excited for you because I know personally how hard the journey can be. But I also know the rewards for faith and determination. You've come through too much, for far too long, and now is not the time to give up. You are almost there. Stay focused, and remember, your breakthrough is up to you.

WHAT YOU SEE IS WHAT YOU GET

At this point, we can almost say for certain that the woman with the issue of blood was scared. But she kept walking. Was she weak? I'm most certain that she was, but with whatever strength she had, she kept going. Was she hurt by all the nasty things people said to her and about her? Probably so in the beginning, but by the time she got in the midst of the crowd, I bet what she was chanting spoke volumes over what they could negatively say about her and to her ever again. She was no longer bound by their words and traditions or the issues of her past because she had a Word about Jesus. She believed it, and she spoke it. Her faith made her see in her mind what she could not yet see with her eyes, and it was propelling her through. It was all or nothing for her, and that stance allowed her to receive her breakthrough. Faith made her breakthrough inevitable. Hebrews 11:6 makes it clear that God is a rewarder of those who believe and diligently seek Him. Don't put God in a box or on the clock. Keep this in mind: momentary setbacks may seem more like a denial rather than just a delay, but let me tell you, I have learned throughout the years that often the biggest opposition comes just before a breakthrough or miracle. Keep moving forward. I'm encouraging you now more than ever to meditate on the promises of God; don't meditate on your problems. The power of Jesus to heal whatever ails you and to help you in every area of your life is within your reach. You, dear lady, have everything you need to draw upon for your breakthrough.

THE TOUCH OF FAITH CHANGES EVERYTHING

Imagine the scene now: the crowd was steadily moving, but it was just so large—so many people. The pushing and shoving was getting out of hand, and people were bumping up against one another, including the disciples and Jesus. But something happened. Over the roar of the crowd and even over the sound of her own chanting, she heard someone call His name: "Jesus." That seemed to incite the crowd, and as the roar of the crowd got louder, they began to rush forward. Harder and harder they pushed, and louder and louder the voices became. It took all her strength to remain upright. Fear began to grip her, but the issue that caused her to be broke could no longer break her spirit. Clearly, the faith she had in what she heard about Jesus could not be broken by the noise or the threat of the crowd. The harder the crowd pushed, the more she chanted to herself: "If I can just touch the hem of His garment, I know I will be made whole."

And then, right there in the midst of that crowd, she saw Him. The moment she had been hoping for, the very scene she had envisioned in her mind and chanted about, had finally come. She was within arm's reach, and with her last ounce of courage, she reached forth and grabbed on to the hem of His garment. She knew right then and there that her life would never be the same, for immediately, she felt it. The source of her issue dried up, and her issue stopped.

THE TOUCH OF FAITH DRAWS JESUS'S ATTENTION

It happened so fast that it appeared nobody knew what had just taken place, and as far as she was concerned, no one needed to know. But her touch was no ordinary touch. It was not just a casual brush against Jesus. It was not a slight touch of His clothes just to be able to say, "I touched Him." It was not an I'll-try-it-and-see touch. Oh no, her touch was not one to go unnoticed; it was purposed, strategic, planned, and backed by her faith. To be sure, her touch was physical—she did grab hold of His garment, and she did feel her issue immediately stop. Here then is a lesson for us: the touch of faith transcends time, space, face, or place and stands solely on the Word of God. Faith draws on the power of Jesus to heal, deliver, and set people free of the bondage to their past and the strongholds of sickness, disease, and sin. He felt it too, and He responded as He turned toward the crowd and asked the question, "Who touched me? Somebody touched me, for I felt power drawn from me." Her touch of faith drew Jesus's attention, but it also proved and exposed His divinity as it drew His healing power, and they both felt it.

Jesus turned to face the crowd to seek her. At first I thought this seemed so unfair that she had come so far and through so much to finally get healed only to end up getting caught. My initial thoughts were, "Would Jesus let her go through all she went through to get her healing and then take it back or allow the crowd to harm her, or worse, kill her? Would He condemn her? After all, legally, she did make Him unclean." She is just a "certain woman" with issues. The answer to those questions is a resounding no! What we discover is that Jesus's response to the touch of this woman is the portrait of the true compassion, grace, mercy, and unconditional love He has for anyone who would come to Him by faith. No, He doesn't want to confront her to condemn her, and He doesn't want to chastise her or to say or do anything to harm her. The Bible says when we come to Jesus full of sickness, troubles, and sin, and we reach for His healing, delivering, and breakthrough power, that Jesus won't brush aside the bruised and the hurt (Isaiah 42:3). In other words, He will show us compassion, comfort us, and respond to us according to our need and His Word. Now that right there is a healing balm all by itself, to know that no matter our issues, sickness, disease, or sin, Jesus will receive us by our faith.

THE TOUCH OF FAITH DRAWS JESUS'S ACCEPTANCE

I believe there is more. Jesus asked who touched Him because He felt the touch of faith draw power from Him. But I believe He also wanted the woman and the crowd to know that He does not discriminate, and that He cannot be soiled or tarnished by our sicknesses, diseases, poverty, sins, or any of the legalistic consequences that were attached to a woman having an issue. You can go to Jesus just as you are, from right where you are. As a matter of fact, throughout the scriptures, Jesus often bid the diseased, sin sick, troubled, and burdened to come unto Him. (Just like He did to me that night when He called to me in the club.) Jesus beckons us to cast all our cares, burdens, problems, and issues on Him. At times Jesus even asked others to bring people to Him who had issues, sickness, disease, and sin, and He healed them (Luke 4:40). All I'm trying to say here is that what that woman had was a Word about Jesus, and when she got ahold of His garment, it was symbolic for getting a grip on His Word, His commandments, and His promises. Remember, God's Word will do just what He said it will do. Believe it, and don't be afraid to reach out to Jesus with your issues or even with your sins. I'm telling you, He can and will turn your life around. He'll heal those hidden hurts, and He'll clean you up from the stain of your past. I can tell you personally that Jesus can make it so you don't even look like what you have been through. Do it now; He will not turn you away. Reach out to Him. Call on His name. I thank God that He will accept you just the way you are. Jesus does not discriminate.

Yes, Jesus asked, "Who touched me?" And then He gave value to the woman's life when He said, "Somebody touched me." Can you imagine the things running through this woman's mind when she heard that? She had lost all her worldly belongings, her self-worth, and her identity because of her issue. She had been called unclean for twelve years, and she began to see herself as others did: untouchable, dirty, unclean. She was cast out of mainstream society and treated like she was a nobody, and now Jesus said, "*Somebody* touched me." It frightened her to the point of trembling with fear, but it also moved her so much that right there in front of the crowd that was judging and condemning her, she fell at His feet in humble reverence. She confessed that she was the one who touched Him and felt His power heal her body. As a matter of fact, touching Jesus was so freeing that she told her entire story for all to hear.

That's just what happened to me that morning after I left that club. After begging Jesus to deliver me from that horrible lifestyle, I knew He had answered my prayer. I knew when I got up off that floor that I was free. I admit it was difficult for me at first to openly tell my story in front of people, especially those whom I drank and drugged with, slept with and partied with. I was afraid of what they would say or even do. I had a friend say to me once when I told him about what God had done for me that a leopard never changes its spots. But I didn't know enough about the Word then to know that whom Jesus sets free is free indeed—no question about it. I ran into that guy just this year at a mutual friend's funeral, and his mouth dropped when, twenty nine years later, from the first time I told him my story until that funeral, he saw me. I felt his eyes on me the entire time he was there. Then he heard me speak. I was, in fact, preaching the eulogy for our friend. He was so humble and so kind. Now this is not about me preaching the eulogy. This is about the fact that God set me free from my behavior and my past. And whatever spots I may have are the residue God uses to either draw people to me whom I can relate to and help, or He uses the spots as reminders to me of where He's brought me from, helping me to keep a grip on His Word.

Now I tell my story everywhere I go. I take advantage of any opportunity I can and tell it to anybody and everybody who will listen. And that's why I'm writing it in this book. God has been too good to me. He saved my life, even when I didn't know to ask Him to save me. The sicknesses and diseases I should have, I don't have. I know Jesus healed me of diseases I didn't even know I had. He made a way for me to pay bills, and I still can't tell you how. And I've seen Him do it in the lives of so many of the women I've met and ministered to along my journey; women who were hurting and dying are now living free of the hurts and anxieties associated with their pasts, their mistakes. And it's all because of faith. There were those who called me names, who said I was nothing and would never be anything. But the devil is a liar. I started believing Jesus, and even though I kept falling, by the grace of God, I kept getting back up. And now those same people call me Reverend Nikki, woman of God, preacher, anointed one, child of the King. Don't get me wrong. I am not boasting in those titles, but I am boasting about the cleansing power and amazing grace of Jesus. Nobody could do that but Jesus. But I had to believe it, and I did. I still believe it. That's break-through faith. That's the kind of faith that gets Jesus's attention. And so, just like I read and heard the story of the woman with the issue of blood and it helped me, I tell my story in the hopes that God will use it to help others get their breakthrough. Get free, free indeed!

THE TOUCH OF FAITH EXPOSES JESUS AS SAVIOR

When she touched Jesus, confessed her faith in Him, and then shared her whole story, she exposed even more than His divinity and His healing power, for when Jesus begins to respond directly to her, He addresses her as "daughter." To me this is so critical because, as discussed earlier, we often take on the names and stigmas attached to our issues and situations until we begin to define ourselves by them. She had been called unclean for twelve years. It was like saying you're a nobody, and you don't have anybody; you don't belong here. I'm certain that many of you reading this book have been called names that are related to your issues. Often, because our issues isolate us and separate us from our biological family relationships, we also lose sight of who we are as well as our sense of belonging, our sense of family. But now, for her, the tables were turning. When she told Jesus her story, when she told Him about her faith, it exposed Him as the Savior, the one who came to give new life to those who believe and have faith in Him (2 Corinthians 5:17). That's why He called her daughter. It was not just a nice thing to say to make her feel good, but it was a heartfelt term of endearment that shows a personal relationship. It represents inclusion, not exclusion. Being unclean had separated her from mainstream society, but being called daughter by Jesus ushered her into the Kingdom of God. She became a child of the Most High God (John 1:12). Jesus said, in essence, "Your issue may have caused you to be rejected by man, but I accept you. I love you. I came for you that you might have life and have it more abundantly. Because of your faith, you are now a part of God's family" (John 3:16). Yes, she got the healing for her body, but Jesus also saved her life forever. When she walked away from that crowd that day, she was assured that even if they did kill her, she would not find herself living in hell forever, but she would be with Jesus in heaven eternally. Hearing this, even if He did not heal her of her sickness and she had died, she would still have had her breakthrough because in heaven there is no sickness, disease, issues, sorrow, or pain (Revelation 21:4).

Her confession reveals that her real point of contact with Jesus was her faith. Yes, she reached out with her hand and touched His garment, but it was her faith that touched His heart and drew the healing and saving power of Jesus. I heard the old folks say when I was a little girl, "Faith is like the electric cord, and Jesus is the outlet. Once you plug into it, you connect to the power source." She certainly had the right hookup. It was her faith that did it. Oh my goodness, I told you there was more to her story than meets the eye. And still it isn't over.

I imagine in the back of her mind she was focusing on how she could safely get out of harm's way. You see, unfortunately, although her issue stopped when she grabbed onto Jesus's garment, according to the law, she was still considered unclean and had to go back into seclusion for seven days. How horrible to know that you are healed but that you still must wait on a manmade law to declare it. The law demanded that on the eighth day she take a sacrificial offering to the local priest, who would offer the sacrifice to God on her behalf. Then the priest would declare her clean. Then and only then could she legally and safely return to mainstream society. Jesus knew all this, yet He would not let her get away.

FAITH EXPOSES JESUS AS HIGH PRIEST AND THE LIVING SACRIFICE

You're probably saying, "Please don't tell me I read all this just to find out that she went through all she did to get healed and saved, but she still walks away considered unclean." Well, ladies, you are right. She is going to walk away healed, and yes, she is walking away saved, but I promise you, there is no need to get discouraged. Jesus is not about to let her leave that crowd with that stigma of being un-clean still attached to her. Oh no. She was blessed coming into that crowd and touching Jesus, and she is about to get blessed even more going out. You see, her touch of faith exposed Jesus as the High Priest (Hebrews 4:15) because after she confessed and told Jesus her story, He declared, "Daughter, your faith has made you well. Go in peace, and be free of your issue." There it is right there. That's her point of breakthrough. She was free from the source of the issue and the stigma and trauma of her past. She didn't need to go get a sac-rifice, and she didn't need to go to a local priest. Her touch of faith exposed Jesus as our High Priest and as our intercessor, for He came to be the living sacrifice (Romans 3:25; Hebrews 18:11–14) once and for all who will believe and come to Him by faith. He lives as our High Priest, the one who declares us clean and free to go.

YOUR FAITH IN JESUS: FAITH EXPOSES HIS FAITHFULNESS TOWARD YOU

Jesus took her beyond the barriers of sickness, of being ostracized and broke. In other words, she had come to the hem of Jesus's garment for physical healing, but her faith took her from the hem to the heart of Jesus. Oh, He healed her, for sure. But He also saved her soul, and He sent her away knowing once and for all that she was made well and that her life would never be the same. "Go in peace," He told her. I believe this is what He meant: "Daughter, you belong to Me now, and so that makes you clean. You can go away from this crowd and never worry about all this again. Go. Not only has your issue stopped but also the source of your issue is dried up. Go knowing that disease and death have no hold over your life any longer. Go knowing that your whole life is changed. Go, daughter, knowing you can go to the temple, sit in the park, and walk down the street with your head up. Go knowing and believing this: I am with you always. I will never leave you or forsake you. You need only to call My name, and I will hear even your faintest cry. Go knowing that no weapons formed against you shall be able to prosper. Go knowing that greater is He who is in you than he who is in the world. Go knowing that I will keep you in perfect peace as long as your mind is grounded in Me, in My Word. Go knowing you are no longer the victim. Go knowing that you have the victory through Christ Jesus. You are victorious! Daughter, your faith has made you well. *You got your breakthrough!*"

I hope you need a minute right now. Can you feel the power in what happened? Are you celebrating with me right now for the woman with the issue of blood? What a journey! What a testimony! All because she heard a Word about Jesus, and she listened. She believed it, she spoke it, and she acted on it. She got a grip on that Word, and when she did—breakthrough!

OK, OK, I know I can just say a prayer and the benediction and end the book right here. And, at first, I said I was not going to tell anybody, but I just can't keep it to myself. There is more to my story.

I'M ON THE RIGHT ROAD NOW
I left off writing about my story after the affair ended in 1995. I must admit that things were really bad for me for a few years, but slowly, they

began to turn around. God restored to me all I had lost and more as He blessed me with a good job, a nice home, and a car—as well as a new church home (First Baptist Church of Glenarden, with Pastor John K. and First Lady Trina Jenkins), where I developed a strong relationship with Jesus as I began learning the Word more intently and applying it to my daily living. I began to look at life differently from how I ever had before. Outside it seemed all was well. God was using me. I was preaching and singing and teaching. But there, in that tender, weak spot, still nagging at my core, was my need to be first. I hid it behind ministry until someone would call me and literally tell me I wasn't their first choice, that they had tried to get so-and-so, but that person(s) was too busy, unavailable, or too expensive. Once again I felt bad and not good enough to be chosen first. Still, I'd say yes. I remained humble before God, because I was so grateful that at least I had been chosen. But I would be hurt, because I wasn't the first choice. Sometimes I would minister out of that hurt, and honestly, out of bitterness. I'd question myself: What's wrong with me? Why do I always have to be the last resort? Then I'd start that cycle all over again of tearing myself apart. I kept telling myself that I wasn't good enough, and I adopted the always-the-bridesmaid-never-the-bride mentality.

I was working full time and involved in ministry in and outside my church. But one night I came to a critical place. I was sitting at my computer doing some studying online when I received a call to sing at an event. The caller said she had asked someone else, but that person's fee was far too expensive. She said she had reminded the event committee that they could count on me. I got angry, I was hurt, and I finally told her how I really felt, and I declined. In the past, I would never have said no.

Please know this: I believe with all my heart that I was born to sing and to preach and to teach the Gospel of Jesus Christ. But I no longer wanted to be people's last-minute "desperate choice." After that phone call with that lady who did not know how to respond to me, I sat at my desk and cried in bitterness, pain, and anger. "God, you said I am the head and not the tail. You said I am your child. God," I cried, "then why can't I just be first? I just want to be first in somebody's life." I revisited my past, and that made me cry so hard and so long from such a deep place of pain that I could hardly catch my breath. I was lonely, feeling like God was punishing me, and it all spilled out. I cried out, "My mommy didn't want me, my daddy didn't want me, and my son's dad didn't want me," and on and on I went. I can admit now that it was the eve of desperate despair. I was at one of the lowest places in my life, and I wanted to die. Even now tears fall easily from my eyes as I write about that night. I know now that my cry was not of a woman but the bottled-up cry of a hurting eight-year-old little girl. Yes, as good as things were in my life, on the inside I was still a mess. I had suppressed it, worked around it, preached over it, and sung through it, but I had not dealt with it, and it finally all came to the place of reckoning. All that was about to come to an end, for in the midst of my breakdown was the threshold to my breakthrough. My crying out, my reaching out to God for delivering me from that awful issue, not only healed my issue but also gave me Words that I could cling to for life.

I could hardly see the keyboard because of my tears. But then I heard it. I heard His voice. Above my crying, I heard that same voice I'd heard on that fateful night in the club in 1989. Yes, it was the voice of God. God had chosen to speak to me again, and as He spoke, I typed these words: "My dearest daughter, you have always been first. Before I tossed a star in the sky, before I caused the sun to shine, I chose you (Ephesians 1:4). Before I formed you in the womb, I knew all about you. I created you on purpose, with purpose (Jeremiah 1:5), before even the foundation of the world. I chose you first. I love you so much that although you were yet a sinner, Jesus died for you (Romans 5:8). I sent my only begotten son to die for you (John 3:16). Daughter, you have always been first."

That was it. God said I have always been first. He called me daughter. I got up from my desk still crying, but this time, they were tears of joy. I held on to those Words. I kept reading them over and over until I was speaking those Words. I got a grip on those Words, and I did not let go until I felt my breakthrough, and right there in my room, that night, I got it. I got my breakthrough.

That's what a Word from God will do if you believe it, speak it, act on it, and get a grip on it. It births joy and humility, but it also gives us victory. I felt the breaking within. I felt the heaviness that I'd carried for so long lifted from my heart. I finally got it.

Jesus said we can cast all our cares on Him, for He cares for us (1 Peter 5:7). As I reached out that night, God responded in a most profound way. From that moment on, I began to see myself as God sees me. He called me daughter. In spite of my wrongs, my weaknesses, I am still his daughter. He chose me first, and nothing and nobody can change that. He loves me unconditionally. I had been first all along. Finally, after all those years, I was free. Having the faith to call on God and believing He would help me drew His attention, acceptance, and assurance, I got it. God was faithful. I got my breakthrough.

Now when I'm not considered first for something, when another year comes and goes, and I am still single while I see others around me meet the men they end up marrying, I wish them well and keep holding on to the Word that reminds me that I am not alone and never will be, for Jesus said He would be with me always, even unto the end of time (Matthew 28:20; Hebrews 13:5). I still hold on to God's Word when someone else gets the job, the raise, or the promotion, and I find out it was between them and me. I learned that what God has for me is for me, and nothing and nobody can take that away. I've grown to be patient, because I know God will come through. He will do just what He says He will do. I still hold on to that Word when I get those calls, and I know I'm not the first choice. I just humble myself and say yes if I'm available, because I am called to be a servant, and God's Word, my story, and my songs are full of hope, strength, power, and the Word that births faith to help others.

Since that fateful night, I've had the opportunity to sing before two US presidents, the governor and county executive of Maryland,

and many more. I've had the opportunity to speak before corporate leaders and church and faith-based dignitaries from around the world. My name, Nikki Pearson, is written in the White House history books. That is an honor I don't take lightly. Only God could make those things happen. God continues to use me and bless me.

In 2001, I received the Woman of Distinction award that has celebrated women such as Oprah Winfrey, J. C. Haywood, and other noted women of color around the country for commitment and dedication to serving family, communities, and the nation.

In 2005, I had the opportunity to move my biological daddy into my home. I loved my daddy still with the heart of an eight-year-old. I took care of him and tried to make whatever time he had left to live his best days. I think in those seven years we got pretty close to that. He and my mother forgave each other and rekindled their friendship, which started a healing in my family three generations deep.

In 2010, I became a catechism student under the tutelage of Pastor Anthony E. Moore, Carolina Missionary Baptist Church, and in 2011, I, W. Nikki Pearson, became an ordained reverend at the First Baptist Church of Glenarden. My daddy, my mom, and my sister were there together. Daddy died the following year. Grief tried to take me back and take me out. It was during that first year of grieving that my mom and I became closer than we'd ever been. I remember so vividly her calling me one evening because she was missing Daddy. After we talked awhile and cried a minute, she told me that she and Daddy were proud of how I had turned my life around. She laughed and said, "Only the good Lord could do that." She called me her baby. That day the little girl in me got her mom back. Mom and I remained close until her untimely death around Christmas in 2016. My heart still grieves deeply for her and daddy, but I thank God once again for turning my life around and for giving me another chance at life. Don't you get it now? Nothing in our life goes to waste with God. He uses everything to make us better, not bitter, and to bring glory and honor to Him.

Now it is 2017, and you are holding in your hand, or reading or listening to via some form of technology, my very own book. This is not about my accomplishments, for surely I know that apart from God, I am and can do nothing. This is about how great, kind, merciful, and faithful God is to take all the hurt and harm and even the wrong from my life and to make me into something good He can use to help others. Now *that* is a breakthrough. All things do work together for the good. I got my breakthrough, and so will you.

Your breakthrough is up to you.

Breakthrough

So, ladies, in every chapter, I have given you scriptures to help instill and develop your faith. I've shared the story of the woman with the issue of blood, and I have been very transparent in telling you the details of my story to further help you to build your faith and to strengthen and sustain you as you take your own personal journey to your breakthrough. I encourage you to read the scriptures out loud and to speak them until they are embedded in your mind and heart. Live by them, and share them with others. And by all means, download or purchase a Holy Bible. I personally like reading the New King James Version (NKJ). Find a good church where the Word of God is preached, taught, and sung with boldness and authority.

Finally, when you get your breakthrough, tell it. Tell your story (Psalm 107:2). Share the scriptures that helped ignite and build your faith. Don't be afraid or ashamed to tell people what God has done for you. It may be just what they need to get their breakthrough. If you find this book has helped you in any way, please purchase one for a friend or family member—or even a perfect stranger. Tell them, "If you want a breakthrough in your life, then get yourself a Word that speaks to your situation. Believe it, speak it, act on it, get a grip on it, and watch it come to pass. Your breakthrough is up to you." God bless you!

Father, thank You for entrusting me to write this book. I pray now that everyone who reads this book will open their hearts and minds to receive the truths of Your Word. I pray that You will guard their hearts and minds as they start their journey to breakthrough. Thank You for Your protection, provision, promises, presence, strength, and power. I speak life and not death unto them. I speak healing and deliverance and breakthrough for each of them. I pray You give them the boldness to proclaim Your Word that equips, encourages, and empowers others to press through their crowds of opposition and on to breakthrough. Thank You for our breakthroughs. You alone deserve all the glory and honor and praise. In Jesus's name, amen.

Author Biography

W. Nikki Pearson, or "Reverend Nikki," is passionate about using sound biblical teaching to encourage others to overcome obstacles and confront their issues. She serves as an associate pastor at First Baptist Church of Glenarden in Maryland and is a Bible instructor and women's group facilitator. She often speaks at women's conferences and retreats, and women's detention centers, and drug and alcohol treatment facilities.

Reverend Nikki embodies determination and faith in all she does—and she hopes to pass that on to those hungry for the power of the Word of God. She knows that the same faith that has brought her through will lead others to their own breakthrough.

Reverend Nikki has one son and three grandchildren. When she's not inspiring others through her celebratory teaching and showing believers how to grow in their faith, she can be found listening to sermons, reading, entertaining, traveling, or spending time at the beach.

Nikki would love to serve as speaker for your women's group, or congregation. If you are interested in scheduling her to speak at your event, teach a workshop, facilitate a focus study, or do an in-person book signing, call 301-318-4396 or send an inquiry to nikkipearson@ live.com.